A SURGICAL APPROACH TO MEAT CUTTING

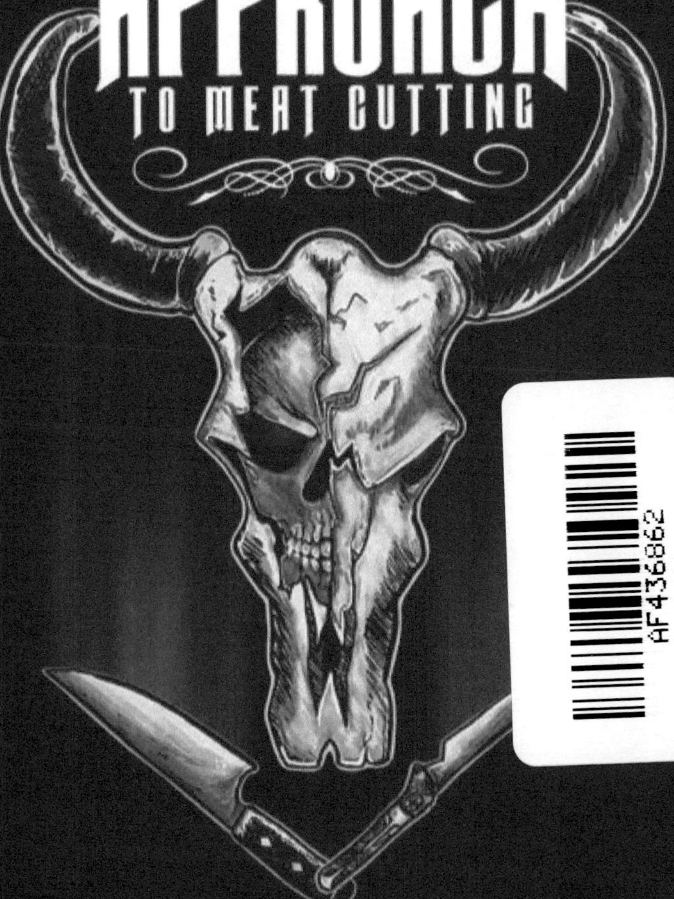

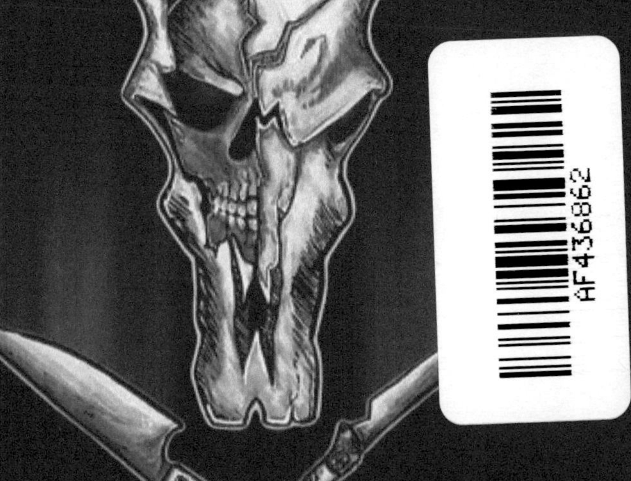

ADAM G. ELLIS

AND

GEORGE F. ELLIS, MD

A SURGICAL APPROACH TO MEAT CUTTING

Cutting, Carving and Cooking for Success

ACKNOWLEDGEMENT

Without the experiences and support from our family, friends, peers, and the team at Clarens Publishing, this book would have been difficult to complete. You have given us the opportunity to accomplish a wonderful journey.

Having some thoughts and turning it into a book may sound easy, but it is not. The experience is challenging, but when completed, it is quite rewarding. I especially want to thank the individuals that helped make this happen. Complete thanks to everyone who has touched our lives and thereby had a hand in finishing this book.

Special thanks to Master Butcher Timothy Lesher for their expertise and contributions and Beth Ann Leonard, our culinary advisor.

Dedicated to Adam's grandparents, Dr. George and Denyse Ellis.

TABLE OF CONTENTS

CHAPTER 1

A SURGICAL APPROACH TO THE CULINARY ARTS

A father who is a surgeon and a son who is a butcher. While we've sometimes been at odds over the years, as any parent and child have, we wanted to create something together.

Our jobs have more similarities than initially meets the eye. To be a surgeon takes patience and exactness. You have to stay on top of every detail as the process goes, and once you make a decision, you can't take it back. In meat cutting and cooking, the same rules apply. And, unlike the body, ingredients and meat can't repair itself. Both careers have required training, dedication, and continued research, as the spheres of medicine and food preparation are ever evolving.

George Ellis, MD, FACS

I trained in Syracuse NY and New Orleans, LA at Tulane, and have worked as a urologist and healthcare administrator in clinical and hospital settings around America. Having earned a Master's Degree in Medical Management from Tulane, I've provided consulting services to hospitals and clinics from the perspectives of Strategic Planning, Finance, and Analysis of Operations. Both Adam and I are close, and are fond of spending time outdoors. One of our favorite winter activities is hiking or skiing, followed by visiting a local eatery or brewery.

Winter sports in general is something I keep up with, as our family spends time in Colorado, visiting Adam's brother, Greg, during the cooler months. What sparked the idea for this cookbook was the Surgical Grand Rounds presentation, "A Surgical Approach to Mount Everest" by a peer who had climbed Mount Everest. He detailed the measures one has to take in order to complete the climb. Akin to a, 'surgical strike,' this is an undertaking that requires precision and planning, as well as commitment to follow it through. I was so fascinated by the title and the presentation as a whole that it got me thinking about my own techniques as a surgeon, and how I apply that to other facets of my life.

Like my son Adam, I love cooking, and it is something we have bonded over as a result. I take my time when preparing meals, and have several recipes that are zen-like in how I go through each step.

Adam Ellis, CNA

I have had wide experience in the healthcare and retail industries, with expertise in management inventory, and organization. I pride myself on always dedicating my professional time to doing a job right while also remaining courteous with those I'm around. I've worked for several national corporations, like Penske and HCA Healthcare, which ignited my entrepreneurial spirit to start and maintain my own online business.

With certifications as both a nursing assistant and food handler, being in service of others and a love of the culinary arts is what led me to join a popular specialty food store. I received extensive training in meat cutting and retail sales, working up the chain to ultimately become one of the store's senior managers. I still hold this position now, and my values haven't changed. In fact, the concepts of good cooking, safety, and timely service continue to motivate me at work, and steer me in my other ventures.

I remember skiing Song Mountain with my brother and cousins near Syracuse, how intimidating it was at first for us all. Like my Dad, I try my best to stay fit; running, hiking with friends, and going to the gym. Eating right is a big part of my routine. When on vacations I crave the experience of local foods and drinks. A trip to Germany for Oktoberfest was where I learned first-hand about hearty food, such as high quality beef, sausage, and schnitzel, as well as the culture of brewing beer.

That adventure led me to obtain my certification as a Cicerone.

We'd be remiss as lovers of food if we didn't mention our favorite places from around the United States. In Florida, beachside dining is a culture all its own. In New Smyrna, one of our local visits near the waves is, The Garlic. With glowing string lights and views of the ocean, we love dining here for upscale Italian food. Their selection of wines from France and Italy pair perfectly.

Flagler Tavern, also in New Smyrna, is a bar and restaurant that has live music and even a steampunk, nautical-styled speakeasy. What we enjoy about this eatery is the variety of dishes they have. There are classic American grill meals, seafood options, plates inspired by Asian cuisine, and tons of alternatives for dietary restrictions. The willingness to try new things on their menu and think outside the box, both with courses and cocktails, is inspiring to us as foodies.

The New Smyrna Brewery has the typical industrial approach to their interior design, but their beers are far from average. With unique names for each brew, and flavors for both trends and more traditional, we love the brewery for its approach to branding and quality. It's a great place to hangout, either one on one, or when we have visitors from out of town who want to enjoy a drink and conversation.

While we live in Florida, Colorado is like our second home. Whether we're enjoying the mountains or the urban areas of the state, there is a list of establishments we frequent every chance we get.

Though we're not near a breach, we still love the waterside. Pug Ryan, a brewery in Dillon, is right near the amphitheater and manmade lake. And, maybe we love it so much because of its tiki bar; a slice of Florida in the middle of the mountains and firs.

The Breckenridge Distillery and Brewery is tucked amongst the trees near a ski lodge and golf club. It's hard not to stop in after a day outdoors, and we often find ourselves pulling up a chair here after a day on the slopes. Breckenridge is one of our favorite brands of whiskey. Not only do they offer tastings, but their restaurant offers custom cocktails showcasing their product. Their appetizers and meals hit the spot when you've worked up an appetite.

Our last recommendation has to be Brasserie 1010, a cozy, Parisian-style restaurant in Boulder. It's a lovely place to unwind for dinner while you people watch downtown. They have a large variety of French dishes, and their wine and cocktail menu accompanies each dish flawlessly; especially when happy hour rolls around.

While our palate always adapts to the vibe of a location, there are some foods we can't help but seek out when our stomachs are growling. We both love meat, so a prime rib, or choice of beef served as a steak or burger is guaranteed to sate us. The beer, wine, or spirit we gravitate toward is often more of a spur of the moment decision.

The journeys that surgery and butchery have taken, with antiquated beginnings and evolutions as time has progressed, are more comparable than not. The efficiency of techniques and the quality of the work people were doing in these fields has improved, all thanks to advancements in technology, as well as general awareness. We have always been fascinated by history, and like those who've come before us, we recognize the need to adapt and continue growing.

One of the tools that has seen the greatest advances is the knife. It seems so simple, yet it's the most obvious implement when you think of all the ways a knife can be used. Knives and other tools for precise, neat cuts are needed in both professions. And, valuable tools need to be maintained. Prep is also a necessary part of cooking, and surgery. A medical procedure is not unlike a recipe. You take everything step by step.

There are three major categories of cooking, dry heat, moist heat, and combination cooking, as well as subcategories. You can prepare one recipe several different ways. Maybe you'll decide to slow cook your meatballs instead of frying them in a pan? Or, perhaps you'll bake them in the oven? Understanding the differences between these methods, and grasping the best ways to cook something, case by case takes time. To become a master in the kitchen requires hours, days, years of dedication. But we all have to start somewhere; the basics of cooking are within arm's reach, so long as you're ready to begin the journey.

Talking about the surgical approach to cooking and not talking about healthy ways of eating would be ignoring the elephant in the room. The more you learn to cook, the more you'll start to learn about the ingredients that you're using. You don't just have to stop at quality control when choosing the foods that go in your fridge. Eating healthy can be a daunting task at first. Everyone has a different budget and each body is different. If there is something specific you're looking to do with your diet, like losing weight or managing symptoms of an illness, we recommend talking to a nutritionist or doctor. However, there are universal foods that are worth incorporating in your diet when possible, and ways to do so that are financially conscious. Frozen or canned vegetables, fruits, and meats may not be the fanciest, but those that come in water (not syrup) are healthier than cups of noodles that are high in sodium. Preparing meals that are nutritionally balanced helps you avoid health complications down the road.

Healthy doesn't mean you have to avoid certain things altogether. There are plenty of things you can enjoy in moderation that are used across recipes, and cultures. Wine, beer, spirits, and cannabis are all examples of this, and ingredients we want to focus on as we love using them for unique dishes.

A glass of wine or beer will often accompany your plate if you've acquired the taste, but they can also bring an earthiness or zest to the meals on your menu. White wines are popular for pasta sauces, while reds are commonly used for steak. You can even use wine to remove caked on sauce or ingredients in a frying pan. Beer is great for sauces, batters, and marinades. One of our favorite inclusions of a lager is our, 'Beer in the Brats,' bratwurst recipe. You don't just have to limit yourself to a porter or chardonnay; what about liquor? Whiskey, gin, vodka, and others are called for when preparing various dishes and desserts.

Our final topic concerns infusion. This process involves brewing drinks and creating meals with dried herbs, berries, or even cannabis.

In this book we will discuss the history of surgery and butchering, cutting techniques, cooking basics, ways to prepare meals with spirits and cannabis, and of course, various recipes we can't help but share.

CHAPTER 2

HISTORY

Why a surgical approach when we're talking about the culinary world? Lord Thurlow observed that, "there is no more science in surgery than in butchering." If kindred methods in both professions hadn't improved, the outlook for public health would be much darker.

The first evidence of a surgical procedure, referred to as *trepanning*, was the act of making a small burr hole in the head. This was practiced as early as 6500 BC and continued well into the Renaissance. The exact reason for this is unknown today, but experts theorize it had more to do with serving a spiritual purpose than a medical one. The ancient Greeks began to hone some surgical skills, learning how to set broken bones, using bloodletting to treat diseases, and draining the lungs if a patient had a respiratory illness like pneumonia. Amputations also began around this time. The Greeks lacked clear knowledge surrounding infections, but made the connection that removal of a decaying limb was a step in the right direction. Even with these archaic advancements, the death toll for the ill was alarming. Much of the information on surgery was attributed to animal dissection. In the 1500s, Ambrose Paré, a French military surgeon, developed cauterization for wounds, and ligating (tying off) blood vessels during amputation to keep a patient from bleeding out.

These breakthroughs, however, did little for the medical world overall. In the early 1800s, nearly half the patients in need of an amputation or resection died in the process. It's no wonder practitioners garnered a reputation as barbarians, unequipped to truly help those with medical needs. Surgery of any kind used to be a brutal and life-threatening affair. A death sentence that was no better than succumbing to complications from the very injury that brought you to the operating table in the first place.

But what made it so dangerous? It wasn't the act of amputation or removal alone. If a surgeon was operating on a limb, they needed to move quickly. Patients were awake for the entire process, with nothing to distract them from the pain other than biting down on a wadded cloth or a bullet. Surgeons thought it was better to rush than subject a wounded soldier to such an agonizing procedure. The average amputation took thirty seconds, with the fastest on record taking only nine. At first, this seemed obvious as an approach. The faster you work, the less blood loss and chance for infection.

Unfortunately, this is horrifyingly untrue. We now know that skill as a surgeon is not about speed or talent with a blade. Medical knowledge acquired over time made it clear that surgery was beneficial, but perfecting it would be the key to success. The early 1800s brought about significant change. There was a time when barbers, because of their skills with a blade, would perform basic medical operations. This was done away with as schools of Medicine in France started focusing on specific areas of the body.

In England, the Royal College of Surgeons began in 1745. Those in the medical field split from the Company of Barber-Surgeons, going so far as to call on an Act of Parliament. The Company of Surgeons was formed thereafter. In 1751, the Surgeons' Hall was built. Problems arose when the company failed to adhere to the rules established by Parliament, and the credibility for the college declined. When the company attempted to get a new Bill of Incorporation, they lost in the House of Lords, and this is where Lord Thurlow delivered his famous line regarding the science of surgery and butchering.

Not willing to accept defeat, the Company of Surgeons made a Petition to the Crown, and were successful. In 1800, the Royal College of Surgeons in London was granted a Royal Charter by King George III. Now those looking to study and improve surgery had a bona fide location to do so.

At this time and alongside England, schools of Medicine in France started focusing on specific areas of the body. Doctors were expected to have a specialized set of skills, rather than holistic ones. Throughout this period, deemed the period of Paris Medicine, doctors learned more about organs, autopsy, and recovery times for patients.

Learning more about the human body was certainly a step forward, but surgery would remain unsafe if a patient couldn't be operated on slowly. And, doing so would be difficult if the patient was awake and unable to stop moving in response to the pain. Concerns of this led to another breakthrough; anesthesia. In 1846, dentist William Morton gave a demonstration at Boston's Massachusetts General Hospital where a surgeon removed a tumor without causing harm. In doing this, they proved that incorporating these drugs routinely for operations was integral to their success.

Surgery became more reliable as the process became methodical.

Physicians from other countries began traveling to Paris to study these methods. The freedom to work more carefully and deliberately not only improved the prognosis for those undergoing surgical procedures, but also strengthened the level of trust and respect the public had for surgeons.

The 19th century saw many successes that laid the foundation for surgeries today. In 1818, the first successful blood transfusion was performed after a woman suffered a postpartum hemorrhage. Joseph Lister, a British surgeon, published the Antiseptic Principle in the Practice of Surgery. This paper broke down the importance of cleanliness during surgery, and the methods needed to mitigate the spread of germs. Eventually, patients in need of more complex procedures like appendectomies and heart surgeries were able to find professional help.

Nowadays, becoming a surgeon is a far more rigorous process. A standard training program can take five to six years to complete, and this is after four years of undergraduate school, followed by another four years of medical school. Some even go on to do additional training. Those specializing in a certain area of the body, such as the brain or kidneys, will study them. Some may even sub-specialize in something for another year or two, receiving formal Fellowship training. In addition, there are multiple phases of certification following training before you can perform surgery. These include: obtaining a medical license in the states where you'll practice, board certification by one of the American Board of Medical Specialties, continuing any education requirements, and optionally applying for membership in the American College of Surgeons. The College was founded in 1910 and is dedicated to improving the care of the surgical patient, and to safeguarding standards of care in an optimal and ethical practice environment. Membership prerequisites are certification by a surgical board of ABMS, two years in active practice, exemplary practice and ethical standards as noted by the local medical community. This requires an application and interview process.

This level of dedication and commitment is a far cry from what was considered expertise in the past.

So where does the art of butchering and meat carving fit in with this? Comparing a surgeon to a professional who cuts up meat to be sold in a shop may seem crude and, to some, sickening. But, Lord Thurlow's comment that, "there is no more science in surgery than in butchering," is not as far off as one might think.

The trade of butchering also has a negative perception. The history of meat and its place in the bellies of societies is also very interesting. As civilization began to urbanize and industrial manufacturing replaced agrarian, where the average person got a top round roast for the dinner table also changed. In America, livestock from the Midwest would be sent to cities where butchers and slaughterhouses would purchase these animals for consumption. This was a messy process, thanks to lack of sewage systems and other sanitary measures. For many years, the meatpacking industry was one known for unhygienic, dangerous conditions. Colloquially, *butchering* something is a way of saying you've ruined it. But this comparison is far from accurate, given how much precision and time goes into perfecting the skill.

Eventually, slaughterhouses were moved out of cities because those in urban areas wanted to avoid the stench. Slaughter took place on the farms, then the meat was transported to butcher shops for city dwellers to peruse. The way livestock was raised and fed, the way meat was packaged, the way it was stored, and the way meals were prepared continued to transform due to modern innovations. Soon, there were mechanisms that provided food and water to cattle. Refrigeration came along, as did faster, reliable modes of transportation.

Meat cutting now had the space to become a more precise, artful affair.

Just as surgeons have a myriad of tools, butchers have different blades like cleavers, boning, carving, and slicing knives each designed for a particular purpose.

Stew meat mostly comes from the tougher parts of animals like cows, elk, deer, or pigs, and comes from the large shoulder of a cow, more commonly called "chuck." But any cut of meat can be used, including roast, top and bottom round, tips, and even high-quality cuts like choice (fillet or rib steak meat) or prime, which is the highest USDA beef grade. Professional meat cutters prefer stew meat coming from the posterior of the animal. This area includes cuts like London Broil, also known as flank steak from the bottom of the cow, or boneless sirloin, which comes from the top. Irish stew is a favorite amongst those who enjoy cooking with beer. A common choice is something like a stout or Guinness.

When you're cooking meat for a stew, a carving knife is the tool most butchers will use. The standard process for preparing meat this way is to cut pieces of stew meat into even-sized portions. While fat does add flavor to the stew, butchers always look to remove any fat that would be excessive.

Professionals who prepare stew beef will usually toss the meat in a bowl, coating it with a mixture of salt, pepper, and flour, evenly coating the pieces with the mixture. After this, the meat needs to be browned.

Our favorite way is sautéing the meat in a pan with a little oil, butter, or bacon grease if you want added flavor. It's always best to do small batches, to avoid too much variation in the browning process. An overcrowded pan can lead to the juices creating too thick of a layer, preventing the beef from forming a crust. Stirring the beef can also affect this, so you want to make sure the meat has a deep crust before turning it in the pan. Once the meat is browned, it's wise to deglaze the pan with something like red wine vinegar, beef broth, or a beer, depending on your recipe. Brown bits left in the pan are full of flavor, so it's best to add them to whatever dish you're preparing.

The motto, *low and slow*, is essential when you're cooking meat. Precision, safety, and timeliness will result in your desired outcome.

This step-by-step approach is one that becomes second nature over time for a professional, not unlike a routine surgery.

Even cutting techniques are similar.

As is described, the long muscle fibers which constitute edible meat would be chewy and more difficult to eat if not cut against the grain.

In surgery, the goal is to access the location of the medical condition that needs to be addressed. Sometimes, the muscle gets cut "with the grain" or parallel to the muscle fibers, so as to minimally disrupt the normal anatomy. However, there are times in order to access the target area the surgeon must cut right through the muscle fiber, which will eventually get repaired with the body's natural healing process. This is usually accomplished by approximating the fascia that envelopes the muscle. This fascia constitutes the strength of the closure and the loose subcutaneous tissue and skin are approximated over the fascia.

Like cutting stew beef, precision, safety, and timeliness will result in your desired outcome, namely a strong closure that will let the patient heal properly. From the perspective of meat cutting, the fascia is called the Epimysium or Silver Skin, which is usually non-desirable by the consumer and is discarded. Thus, the contrast here of the same part of the anatomy which is essential for the desired outcome of the surgeon and is actually discarded by the meat cutter.

Both professions require patience, rather than working in haste. Moreover, being skilled as a butcher or surgeon doesn't entail just memorizing techniques, but having enough of an understanding of the trade to be flexible when resources or circumstances change.

In surgery, there are planned changes, and those that occur during the course of the procedure. For example, a urologist may have an endoscopic approach for a kidney stone that does not require cutting to create an incision, but if there is a technical difficulty, then a skin incision may be needed to remove the stone. If there is a complication or injury to an adjacent organ, this may call for a different approach, or require repair by a surgeon of a different specialty.

For meat cutting, a classic example of changing a technique for the consumer is when a certain cut of meat is requested, and then it needs to be diced, so it's more amenable for a stew. A chef's knife or utility knife would then be used. Alternatively, a carving knife might be used to cube meat that typically requires low temperature and slow cooking time, so they're nice and tender. This is why cooking a stew can use a mixture of bits and pieces left over from cutting up larger cuts of meat into steaks and roasts.

What were once two facets of society that were disorderly and hazardous are now indispensable when we're discussing modern comforts. Our physical condition and diet are predominant forces that shape our decisions. We want a filling meal on our table, and we want to lead healthy lives.

While comparing surgery to meat cutting seems like an odd choice, we've come to recognize the similarities, and will continue to marry these topics throughout this book.

CHAPTER 3

KNIFE TO TABLE

The oldest known knife is 2.5 million years old and is called the oldowan and was used as a weapon, a tool, and for eating. Originally made of flint, copper, or stone, this knife is far cruder in appearance than those we have today. But these ancient tools used by cavemen evolved, and over the course of time, the oldowan progressed into the knife we'd recognize today; being made of stronger materials like steel and iron, and possessing a handle for a more reliable grip. Today's use of knives or any cutting instrument requires training, skill, experience, and good judgment. In this chapter, we will discuss aspects of cutting for food preparation, and the similarities and differences when using cutting instruments for surgical procedures.

When professional meat cutters or chefs prepare food for consumption, there is a safe, rapid technique for slicing and dicing. It's mesmerizing to watch, and learning these techniques requires years of practice and training. A chef's knife must be held correctly. The act of cutting and the cutting action must be accurate in order to have meals that are presented in an acceptable manner. Ideally, both hands must be used to prepare vegetables or meat: one hand to cut, the other to stabilize your ingredients to avoid inaccurate cuts or injuries.

Safety is essential when selecting and using knives. One might think that a very sharp blade is dangerous. In actuality, a knife that is properly improves safety by being more efficient. You're less likely to slip up than you would with a blade that's worn down. A sharpening steel should be used on an ongoing basis during the meat cutting process.

Similar precautions must be taken during many surgical procedures. Often, these are a combination of traction, counter-traction, and cutting along with the optimal exposure of the target organs that will be removed, treated, or reconstructed.

Throughout the course of surgical procedures, scalpels are often disposable thereby eliminating the need for sharpening. However, some surgical instruments are reusable and require maintenance. Scissors for example, like metzenbaum or mayo scissors used for dissection, iris scissors used for delicate cuts, and suture scissors used for removing stitches, need to be routinely sharpened to reduce the chance of a surgeon making a mistake.

So, what are the different types of knives?

- **Boning knives** tend to be slightly thicker and stiffer, and are used in a slicing or dagger motion. Boning knives have a thin tip, and are used to get into joints to cut them. Many meat cutters may use this knife and the fillet knife 80% of the time they're in the kitchen. fillet knives are both thinner and more flexible than most other knives. A blade usually measures between 5 and 9 inches. They feature a prominent upward curve along the blade and a sharp, bended tip.

- **A designated fillet knife** offers the length of a chef's knife, but with the precision of a paring knife. Featuring this exceptionally sharp, thin blade, fillet knives are able to slice effortlessly through meat, allowing for exact cuts along the bone to minimize waste.

- **Slicing knives** allow thin cuts of meat to be made for ham or prosciutto.

- **Breaking knives** are used to turn large pieces of meat into smaller, portioned pieces. These include the skinning knife, scimitar, and the cleaver. The cleaver can be used in association with a mallet in order to avoid slamming the cleaver to make the cut. The cleaver is positioned at the selected location of the meat and the mallet "hammers" the cleaver to complete the cut. In addition, there are larger knives weighing several pounds that are specific to the animal such as lamb splitter, pig splitter and the largest being the two handled beef splitter. They are used in a way that is similar to splitting wood to separate the carcass of the animal into two or more pieces.

- **The ham spoon** is used for removing the femur bone from a cured ham, but can also be used for fresh meat. Its design is a longitudinal curve with a very sharp tip to remove the bone so as to be able to slice the meat.

What about fruits and vegetables?

The main methods of cutting fruits and vegetables are julienne (dice), chiffonade (shredding), slicing, brunoise (fine dice) and mincing. Classic examples of ingredients you use these methods on are pears, apples, zucchini, carrots, onions, and peppers. But where do they truly differ? Isn't this all, just, cutting up food?

Well...

1. **Mincing** is considered very fine cutting, ideal for garlic or other aromatics you're adding to a dish. If you want the flavor more evenly distributed throughout, mincing keeps something like garlic from overpowering each bite of food. Mincing knives tend to have wider blades, which may also be used for crushing. Another technique when you're cooking with garlic, ginger root,

or chili peppers, a wide blade is used to press these ingredients in lieu of a mortar and pestle.

2. **Chopping** is cutting your fruit, vegetable, or herb into a dice without trying to be specific about the shape and size of each piece. This method can be small and rough, and is great when working with parsley, thyme, and rosemary. Ingredients that aren't necessarily visible on the plate, but there in order to add flavor to a sauce, seasoning, or broth.

3. **Chiffonade**, or the French word for crumpling, is when you cut vegetable leaves into long, thin, fine strips or ribbons. These shredded leaves from scallions, or ingredients like basil, swiss chard, and spinach, are commonly used for things such as flatbreads or crepes. To do a chiffonade, you gather the leaves into a stack or roll them together, then slice them lengthwise into the number of strips you desire.

4. **Wedges** are a way to cut fruits and veggies into segments, first by removing the ends, then cutting in the middle to make even shapes.

5. **Parallel cutting** is used to cut broad, thin slices. Just as the name suggests, you accomplish this cut by laying food flat on a cutting board, then angling your knife parallel to the board. This technique is often used for vegetables and meat.

6. **Julienne**, or allumette cuts, are used to create a matchstick shape with fruits or vegetables. Typically reduced to 1.5 mm for the width and 5cm long, julienne is done by cutting ends off a carrot, for example. Then, making a small rectangle before cutting it lengthwise into matchsticks. An allumette cut creates very small matchsticks. The size is a width of 3×3 mm and a length of 5 cm. The technique is used on solid vegetables, such as potatoes, celery, carrots, and pepper.

7. **Jardiniere** is a thicker version of the julienne cut. This is typically used for vegetables that end up in stir fry, ramen, or soups. Or, this may be used when you're prepping food for a side dish. The sizes for matchsticks here range from 2 cm by 4 mm, to 4 cm by 10 mm.

8. **Bâtonnet**, or stick, is the largest cut for crudites or vegetable sides, though not as common. For this technique, you must peel and wash your vegetable of choice, then regularize its shape. Turn it into a rectangle or square by topping and tailing it, and squaring off the sides. Then cut it into 6 cm long pieces, before cutting each of those pieces into 6mm thick slices. In the end, the size tends to be 13×13 mm wide and 5 to 8 cm in length.

There are subcategories of some of these major methods, such as fine or rough shredding or small and large dicing. Each one has a specific use, although some can be interchangeable.

Now let's talk about meat.

We would be remiss if we didn't discuss sausage making. Similar to the medical field, this has been viewed as both an art and form of science for centuries. Closing the skin after surgery can be done in several different ways depending on the experience and judgment of the surgeon. A meat cutter will take scraps and create something delicious. Mathematics is involved when it comes to the ratios of ingredients to assemble and cook sausages.

The type of sausage ranges from breakfast patties to hot dogs, bratwurst to jerky, mild italian to andouille, each with their own method of preparation and content to satisfy someone's taste buds.

What are the most popular types?

1. **Chorizo**, typically called the Mexican sausage here in the United States, is bursting with lots of flavor – chilies, spices, and garlic. If you like hot and spicy, this is the type of sausage you're looking for.

2. **Italian sausages** come in both spicy or sweet (mild) flavors, making it one of the few versatile options on the market. The only difference between the two is spicy sausages come with red pepper flakes, mild do without.

3. **Andouille sausage** is another spicy sausage that is packed with cajun seasonings, often used in gumbo and jambalaya.

4. **Kielbasa** is a Polish, pork country sausage that you can find either smoked or unsmoked. It's typically served with something like sauerkraut or cabbage.

5. **The ever popular Bratwurst**, this sausage is seasoned with salt, ginger, and nutmeg. It's best known in America for being a great tailgating meal, perhaps at a football game or at the racetrack.

The ingredients and tools you typically use are: meats, curing salt, seasonings, sausage casings, a meat grinder, a meat thermometer, a sausage stuffer, smoker, a drying chamber, a kitchen scale, a food processor, and a freezer. But, note that not all of these things are needed to make a delicious sausage.

There are several how to's for making sausage that we want to go over.

Preparation

Everything needs to be chilled and the meat partially frozen. You never want your sausage to get warm, so always keep everything chilled, even the equipment. The temperature in a butcher's room is kept at around 37 degrees Fahrenheit, never exceeding 50 degrees. Casings are best prepared the night before by soaking them in hot water to make them soft. Spices can be combined for the desired seasoning either the night before or the day of.

Mixing & Grinding

Cut up the meat into pieces that are about 1 inch in size, and save the fat to keep the sausage juicy in the end. Follow it up by mixing in the seasonings, salt, and any extra fat you have in a bowl. Then, wrap the bowl with plastic wrap and put it back into the freezer for about 30 minutes. The meat should be chilled, but not frozen. When you're ready to grind the meat up, load in the sausage mixture. There are a few plates you can choose from; fine, coarse, or somewhere in between. You'll then want to place a chilled pan at the opposite end of the grinder where the meat comes out. During this process, it is best to alternate back and forth between meat and fatback (if you're using extra fat), and it's always best to grind at a slower speed than a faster one. Once everything is grounded, additional seasonings or salts can be stirred in.

Casing & Stuffing

Professional sausage making tends to be a bit more complex. It requires skill and tedious steps to create some great textures and flavors. Most suggest you place casings under running water to open them up and remove excess salt or debris. A common practice is soaking the casings in warm water overnight to keep them soft, then rinsing them out with cold water. A sausage stuffer is more efficient than filling each casing by hand, so this tool is a staple in professional kitchens. The casing is placed over the sausage stuffer, with one to two inches hanging off the end. Once this end is tied off, the meat is then slowly pumped through the stuffer until you have a full sausage.

Cooking & Smoking

After the sausages have chilled overnight, your art project is ready to be cooked up! Pan seared, grilled, fried, smoking, any approach will do. A universal rule when cooking sausage, however, is carefully at a lower temperature. All in all, from preparation to table, you'll need about 2-3 days of time. But, the old saying rings true; slow and steady wins the race.

Drying It

A final tactic worth mentioning is drying sausages. This is the path taken when you're trying to make beef jerky. The longest of our processes mentioned, you'll need a drying rack or chamber. The humidity should be at about 70%, while the room temperature can not exceed 50 degrees Fahrenheit or fall below 40 degrees. Drying time can take 3 to 10 hours depending on your temperature. The lower the temperature, the longer the duration. A good smoker can also be used to make jerky.

What are our top tips for making sausage?

1. *Texture is key*. Sausage consists of four main components: meat, salt, liquid, fat. Each ingredient used in different ratios will create different textures. For example, more fat will lead to a smooth, hot dog texture. With trial and error, eventually you'll find the master ratio for each texture you want to achieve.

2. *Keep the meat cold*. Doing this for your sausages and tools will actually preserve the meat's cells. This yields that juicy flavor and texture later on. Professionals often keep grinders and stuffers cool too when making sausages.

3. *Have the right tools for the job*. Each step is so vital. Anything you do to the sausage that isn't deemed "OK" could potentially ruin the flavor. It's important to keep the cell structure of the meat, so buying the perfect grinder with sharp blades, then maintaining them is key here.

4. ***As always, safety requires proper cooking***. From frying to baking, you want to cook slower and lower – not fast and high. The first method allows the meat to be juicy, tender and moist, yet firm enough for that 'snap' you want when you bite into it. Rushing through can cause the sausage to expand and burst, it will dry out or even burn.

In summary, when you're making and cooking your own sausages, except that it isn't a process you're going to master overnight. But, with attention to detail and patience, it's safe to say you'll feel a great sense of pride when you can serve your friends and family an inviting meal. Strive to purchase meat with some fat on it, as no fat can make a sausage dry and flaky. Always sanitize the area you're working in. Your countertops should be spotless, and your grinder and tools need to be cleaned regularly because you're working with raw meat. Our recommendation is using a gallon of cold water mixed with a tablespoon of bleach. Clean the absolute heck out of everything before you use it.

What are our favorite dishes that use these techniques?

BLT CHICKEN SALAD

There are so many versions of chicken salad. BLT Chicken Salad is a combination of 2 deli favorites and is for those who want a salad instead of a sandwich and can be made in a very healthy version. This is a prime example of one dish that includes many cutting skills like slicing, dicing, mincing, chop and manual crumbling. The basic elements of a chicken salad—cooked chicken, mayo, and celery—are mixed with bacon, tomato, lettuce and avocado. Healthy substitutes are written in parentheses.

Ingredients

- 5 slices bacon (replace with turkey bacon)
- 3 cups chicken, diced and cooked
- 1 cup fresh tomato, chopped
- 2 stalks celery, thinly sliced
- 3/4 cup mayonnaise (replace with plain yogurt, hummus or sour cream)
- 2 tablespoons green onion, minced
- 1 tablespoon parsley, chopped
- 1 teaspoon lemon juice
- 1/8 teaspoon Worcestershire sauce, more to taste
- salt, to taste
- ground black pepper, to taste
- 12 leaves romaine lettuce, optional, for serving
- 1 large avocado, optional, sliced, for serving

Steps

1. Cook the bacon in a skillet over medium heat until evenly browned, about 10 minutes, flipping once. Remove the bacon from the skillet to a plate with a paper towel on it to drain and excess oil. Crumble the bacon into pieces.

2. In a mixing bowl, combine the chicken, bacon bits, tomato, and celery.

3. In a separate bowl, combine the mayonnaise, parsley, green onions, lemon, Worcestershire sauce, salt, and black pepper until smooth. Pour the mayo mixture over the chicken mixture and coat well.

4. Refrigerate until cold, at least 30 minutes.

5. Garnish with avocado and serve over a bed of romaine lettuce. You can also serve it with crackers or as a sandwich, if preferred.

CHAPTER 4

COOKING BASICS

Most ingredients in cooking come from living things. Vegetables, fruits, grains, nuts, and herbs, come from plants. Meat, eggs, and dairy products come from animals. Fungi, such as mushrooms and yeast, are used in cooking. While not living, minerals like salt come from our earth, and are common at the dinner table. Few dishes are prepared without water. Even spirits like beer and wine are added during preparation to enhance flavors.

Justin Quek is an award-winning chef from Singapore who specializes in Franco-Asian cuisine. In his words, building skills in the culinary world starts with learning three basic things:

"First, knife skills. Then, knowing how to control heat. Most important is choosing the right product ... the rest is simple."

We've talked about knife skills. Herein, we will further discuss cooking methods.

The three major categories of cooking are: dry heat cooking, moist heat cooking, and combination cooking. There are various subcategories, such as braising, stewing, grilling, and steaming. Whether you're aspiring to be a great chef or an at-home cook, these skills are essential building blocks.

However, before discussing the preparation of food with heat, there are some that don't require heat at all. These are dishes that are essentially served raw, prepared with seasoning and other components that "cook" them, or make them more palatable. Examples that come to mind are raw oysters, ceviche, and steak tartare, also known in Europe as Filet American.

Raw oysters are shucked (opened) and served immediately with combinations of lemon, horseradish, cocktail sauce, or hot sauce. Care must be taken to maintain the oysters' appropriate temperature, from ocean harvest, to storage, to the time they are ready to eat.

Ceviche is a classic no-cook summer dish and can be made with any mild fresh fish filet, like halibut or snapper. It is also commonly prepared with shrimp. It requires a four-hour marinade of the fish with one-and-a-half to two cups of lime juice. This process is what "cooks" the fish. Afterwards, the fish is tossed with plenty of tomatoes, onion, green chiles, olives, cilantro, and avocado, providing a fresh overall flavor.

Finally, steak tartare is also a dish served raw and goes back to Mongol warriors—called Tatar, or Tartars- who tenderized meat under their saddles, then ate it raw. This story was popularized by the French chronicler Jean de Joinville in the 13th century, although he never actually encountered Mongols himself, instead using this as a way of showing that the Tatars were uncivilized. It is also possible that this story was a confusion from an old medical treatment using thin slices of meat to protect saddle sores from further rubbing. Nevertheless, not only is preparing meat in this way *civilized*, it is delicious. The preparation consists of raw ground (minced) meat, usually beef or horsemeat. It's served alongside capers, onions, salt, pepper, and even mushrooms. Some recipes call for Worcestershire sauce and a raw egg yolk to be served on top. Health considerations are such that the meat storage and preparation require you to immediately consume steak tartare after it is made. Freezing the meat for 48 hours is the safest approach to prevent infection by parasites and bacteria.

Now, let's dive into cooking methods.

First, dry heat cooking.

Dry heat cooking refers to broiling, roasting, grilling, baking, and sautéing. These are well known to most chefs and are conducted without any moisture, broth, or water. Dry heat cooking relies on the circulation of hot air, or contact with fat to transmit heat to the food. The ambient temperature of 300 degrees or more is used to create browning; chemical components such as amino acids and sugars turn brown, yielding a distinct aroma and flavor. Think toasted bread.

Next up, broiling.

This is a process where extremely high, radiant heat is used. It's often directed from above the food, cooking one side at a time. Care must be taken to monitor cook times, as browning happens quickly, sealing in juices and flavors before creating a crisp exterior. When broiling, here are some of the best cuts or types of meat to look for:

1. For beef and pork, thinner cuts like steaks, pork chops, or hamburger patties.

2. For poultry, use chicken or turkey cutlets, breast halves, quarters, and legs in the broiler.

3. For fish, thick, sturdy fish like salmon, can handle heat and won't dry out easily.

4. For fruits and veggies, broiling can even be used on fruits and vegetables, such as peaches, grapefruit, asparagus, and brussels sprouts.

How about grilling?

Grilling also uses radiant heat, like broiling, to cook foods quickly and uses equipment with an open grate, but the heat source is located beneath the food. Flipping is required to cook foods on both sides properly, with the distinctive grill marks from the hot surface being desirable. The best foods for grilling are:

1. For burgers, ground meat is moist and grills nicely because the high heat sears the outside of the patty, creating a charred flavor.

2. For other meats like steak or pork, using tender cuts of meat or marinating the meat is best, as grilling removes moisture. Higher fat content and marbled meat like ribeyes, porterhouses, t-bones, and strip steaks produce a succulent grilled steak.

3. With poultry, boneless chicken grills evenly and spatchcocking, or butterflying, of whole chickens helps in the cooking process because they will grill more evenly.

4. Finally, with fish, salmon, tuna, and swordfish steaks are sturdy enough for the grill. Wrapping the fish in foil prevents it from falling through the grates.

Let's talk about roasting.

Roasting cooks the meat from all sides for even browning and is done using indirect heat, usually in an oven. The cooking is slow and coaxes the flavors out of the meats and vegetables. Tender meat is roasted at high temperature, up to 450 degrees, for short periods. For tougher meats, longer periods at 200 - 350 degrees are best. What foods are great for roasting?

1. For meats, roast large cuts of meat slowly and evenly, like pork butt or shoulder, prime rib, and beef tenderloin.

2. When it comes to poultry, whole chickens or turkeys can be placed in a roasting pan or on a rotisserie spit and cooked for several hours.

3. With fruits and veggies, roasting brings out the best qualities in grapes, cherries, tomatoes, pumpkin, squash, eggplant, and cauliflower.

Now, onto baking.

Like roasting, baking uses indirect heat to cook from all sides, but baking is used when making bread, rolls, and cakes, and is usually performed at lower temperatures than roasting. Baking transforms moist dough or batter into a firm product like bread, pastries, and cakes. Another prime example is pizza, which is baked in an oven, transforming the dough into a firm crust and the cheese into melted goodness.

Last but not least, sautéing.

Sauté is a French word that translates to "jump." Sautéing is the act of cooking or browning in a hot, shallow pan and with a small amount of butter, oil, or fat to evenly coat the food. This is a rapid process which requires tossing or flipping the contents of the pan. We'd recommend oiling and heating the pan before adding food, and avoiding overcrowding said pan with too many ingredients. Here are the best foods for sautéing:

1. For beef and pork, tender meats such as ground beef, small, uniform-sized tenderloin, or medallions work well in a sauté pan.

2. For poultry, sautéing sears in the flavor of boneless breasts, or strips, very well.

3. Lastly, vegetables like zucchini, squash, and leafy greens in olive oil and/or butter are great as side dishes. Carrots, celery, and onions often make a flavorful base for other dishes. This latter combination is a well-known French cooking technique, mirepoix, and is also used for roasting meat and providing a base.

Second, moist heat cooking.

Moist heat cooking uses the presence of liquid or steam to cook foods. It's often used to make healthier dishes because it eliminates the need for added fats or oils. The liquid tenderizes the muscle and other fibers in certain cuts of meat, like beef chuck or brisket. It also tenderizes fibrous vegetables and legumes. Unlike dry heat, it will not produce a browned crust.

One of the first subcategories is poaching.

Poaching gently cooks foods in hot liquid, like boiling water, between 140 degrees and 180 degrees Fahrenheit. It's ideal for delicate items to preserve moisture and flavor without other ingredients like oil. Here are the best foods for poaching:

1. *Eggs:* poaching is a common method of cooking eggs that results in a soft, tender white and creamy yolk.

2. *Poultry:* broth, wine, or aromatics can be used as a poaching liquid, which adds flavor to boneless, skinless chicken breasts and making them tender. This chicken can then be cubed, sliced, or shredded and added to salads, pasta, or sandwiches.

3. *Fish:* poaching is a great way to preserve the delicate texture of light fish like tilapia, cod, and sole.

4. *Fruit:* poaching fruits like pears or apples creates a unique flavor and softens it.

Our next category is Simmering.

Simmering is also a gentle process and uses higher temperatures than poaching, usually between 180 degrees and 205 degrees Fahrenheit. Water needs to be brought to a boiling point, then the temperature is lowered to a simmer. Here are our favorite foods to simmer:

1. ***Rice:*** simmering produces cooked rice with a light, fluffy texture.

2. ***Meats:*** tougher cuts, like a chuck roast will release fat and collagen as they simmer.

3. ***Soups and stocks:*** simmering releases the fat and proteins from meat, thereby making a rich flavorful broth for soups or stews.

4. ***Vegetables:*** simmering will soften tough root vegetables like potatoes and carrots.

5. ***Grains:*** grains like quinoa, oats, or millet can be simmered until they reach a soft, edible texture.

6. ***Legumes:*** grains, dry beans, and legumes can be simmered to achieve a softer texture. Cooking times vary depending on the type of beans used.

Next up, boiling.

Boiling involves submerging food in water that has been heated to 212 degrees Fahrenheit. The large bubbles that are produced keep foods in motion while they cook. Slow boil means that the water has just started to produce slow-moving bubbles, but is not at a rolling boil. Here are a few foods that boil best:

1. ***For pasta***, use hot water to cook it quickly, then remove it from the water before the starches break down.

2. ***With eggs***, boiling them in their shells produces hard- or soft-boiled eggs. The hardness of the yolk depends on how long the egg is submerged in boiling water.

3. ***Vegetables:*** Again, tough root vegetables like potatoes and carrots will cook more quickly in boiling water. Test the tenderness with a fork to avoid overcooking.

Finally, let's discuss steaming.

This method uses boiled water that continuously produces a steady steam, which envelops the foods and cooks them evenly, ensuring they retain moisture. So what ingredients are great steamed?

1. **Vegetables:** most vegetables can be steamed with great results.
2. **Fish and Shellfish:** water, broth, or wine can be used when steaming fish, yielding a soft, creamy texture. Things like clams, mussels, lobster, or crabs are cooked inside their shells but will stay tender.
3. **Desserts:** crème brûlée, flan, and panna cotta are all custards made by steaming.
4. **Tamales:** Tamales are a popular Spanish food made by steaming masa, a dough made of ground corn, and fillings inside a corn husk packet like potatoes or beef.

Third, Combination Cooking

Combination cooking utilizes both dry and moist cooking methods. Foods are cooked in liquids at low heat for an extended period, resulting in a fork-tender product. This technique works with the toughest cuts of meat, gradually breaking down fibers until they melt into the liquid. Braising and stewing are good examples of combination cooking.

So, what is braising?

Foods are first seared in an oiled pan then transferred to a larger pot, where it cooks in a small amount of liquid such as water, broth, or stock. Food softens under low heat over time, and the liquid becomes reduced with intensified flavors. Braising is a great method for producing meats that fall off the bone. What can we recommend for braising?

1. *Meats:* tougher cuts of meat, such as pork butt, chuck roast, or lamb are irresistible when braised..

2. *Vegetables:* Vegetables such as potatoes, turnips, and fennel can be braised along with meat for added flavor, or they can be braised alone as their own dish.

3. *Legumes:* Lentils, chickpeas, and green beans can be braised in broth or wine for a texture that's soft but not mushy.

Now, how about stewing?

Stewing is when foods are fully submerged in hot liquid, not partially. Smaller cuts of meat are used in a stew, but the method of slow cooking at a lower heat is the same. Fibrous vegetables break down and fat and collagen from the meats melt away, resulting in a thick, flavorful gravy filled with tender bites of meat and veggies. Here are our recommendations for stewing:

1. *Meats:* Meats that are rich in collagen and fat do well in a stew pot. This includes briskets, oxtail, or chuck roast.

2. *Vegetables:* Vegetables add depth to your stews, so the use of onions, carrots, potatoes, celery, parsnips, turnips, or rutabaga is recommended. These vegetables all either enhance the flavors of the stew, or easily take on those that have been added.

Here is one of our favorite combination cooking recipes:

SMOKED PORK CHILI

Smoked Pork Chili. This includes smoking meat and sautéing. This tender smoked pork and bacon really makes a difference, and packs the dish full of protein.

Ingredients;

Main Dish

- 2 lbs. pulled or cut pork
- 4 pieces thick cut bacon
- 1 large onion
- 1 red bell pepper
- 1 green bell pepper
- 1, 28 oz. can diced tomatoes
- 2, 15 oz. cans of pinto and/or kidney beans
- 1, 6 oz. can tomato paste
- 2 cloves garlic or 1 tsp garlic powder

Pork Rub

- 2 tbsp vegetable oil
- 1/3 cup brown sugar
- 2 tsp coarse pepper
- 6 tbsp chili powder
- 1 tsp red pepper flakes
- 1/2 tbsp cumin
- 2 tsp oregano
- 12 oz. stout beer

Steps;

1. Plan on starting the day early or smoke the pork the day prior, so it's ready for cutting (or pulling) and simmering.

2. The pork tenderloin can be smoked using an electric smoker like a Bradley Smoker, Masterbuilt, or a Kamado Grill, like a Big Green Egg. Use any commercially available rub and use wood in the smoker, like maple, applewood, hickory and optionally add up to 25 percent oak. The process of smoking will take about three hours.

- ☛ Start the smoker, using wood of choice, setting the temperature of the smoker for 225oF.
- ☛ Trim pork tenderloin of any fat or silver skin.
- ☛ Generously rub the spice mix and brown sugar all over the meat.
- ☛ Place meat in the smoker and smoke till the internal temperature is 145 – 160oF, about 2 1/2 to 3 hours. Allow the meat to rest at least 30 minutes at room temperature. Cut the pork into small 1/2-inch cubes or shred the pork using the pull method.

3. Take a large pot and place on the stove top and add oil and heat on medium/high. Coarsely chop the onion and bacon and place them in the pot, along with coarsely chopped bell peppers and minced garlic until ingredients are translucent but not browned. Next, add the 28 oz. can of diced tomatoes and the 6 oz. can of tomato paste. The next step is to add the spices. You will need to measure and add 6 tbsp chili powder, 1/2 tbsp cumin, 1 tsp red pepper flakes, 2 tsp oregano, and 2 tsp coarse ground black pepper. Add more or less of the spices depending on how spicy you like your chili. Also add salt as needed, depending on periodic tasting during the simmer process.

4. Add in the 28 oz. can of dark red kidney beans and 2 15 oz. cans of pinto beans. Make sure to rinse the beans. We want beans with good hygiene. Once the beans are clean, put them in the pot and add 1/2 bottle of stout beer. Reduce the temperature to medium/low, so that the liquid is barely bubbling.

5. Mix the contents of the pot but do not add the pork yet and allow the mixture to simmer for at least 30 minutes. Once the mixture is satisfactory to the taste, add the pork and make sure to stir the chili every 20 minutes for the duration of the simmer. The final taste test will determine when the chili is finished but usually will take an hour of simmering.

Skills in food preparation are ones you develop over time, like most things through trial and error. You must choose the right meals for your target audience, and they need to be prepared in a safe, timely manner. During surgery, the patient selection for a given procedure is essential; you must consider the nature of the procedure and the general health of the patient. The precision and timeliness of preoperative planning is what helps you accomplish this task.

CHAPTER 5

COOKING HEALTHY

The choices we make regarding our health, both physically and mentally, have a great impact on our lives. We're responsible for the things that will either help or hinder our lives; choosing what we consume, our daily activities, and our overall lifestyle. The types of meals we make, and the way we prepare them, can play a positive role in health maintenance and even disease prevention. Conversely, there are ways we eat that can have a negative influence. Chronic medical conditions such as type 2 diabetes, obesity, and high blood pressure are struggles that should spur those afflicted to wisely consider their diet. Making sure they're eating in a way that is optimal for the management and treatment of their conditions. Even if you don't manage a chronic condition, it is still best to take care of yourself via your diet. This improves your chances of avoiding health complications in the future.

From the perspective of surgery, although complications can arise from surgery in any patient, those who undergo procedures who are in good health have a lower probability of suffering complications. The type of anesthetic used, the general approach to the procedure, and recovery all need to be considered, and these considerations are based on the health of said patient. Chronic illnesses and medications taken on an ongoing basis will affect the treatment choice and outcome of surgery. All this plays into precision, safety, timeliness.

The same can be said of the food choices we make. The quality and quantity of our food, and method of preparation. Planning meals, focusing on specific food groups, limiting excess, and reflecting on nutritional goals are key in leading a healthy lifestyle when cooking.

Planning

"Plans are nothing; planning is everything." Thank you, Dwight D. Eisenhower. If you want to improve your diet, it's okay if you're overwhelmed at the start. There are thousands of trends out there, meal plans, and goals that you'll run into at the start of your journey. Finding the right one for you and sticking to it will take time. You'll need to stay optimistic and dedicated, and it's normal for the first steps of the journey to be the hardest.

Having a plan will make everything easier.

This planning can include writing down a detailed menu and shopping list for the upcoming week. Or notes for a set routine, with a workout and then a taco night. The best advice is to start small. Don't put pressure on yourself to suddenly start going to the gym every day and only eating a limited amount of food. Rather than running a mile through on the first day, accept that you may only run ¾ of that mile and then you'll walk the rest, but that is still a significant step toward your goal. You don't have to make wildly intricate meals to feed your body well. If you're unsure which plans will work best for you, consider looking into working with a nutritionist. While there are some foods that are universally healthy, others are best for specific goals like weight loss, building muscle, and/or improving deficiencies.

If you're not set on making plans, you'll be setting yourself up for confusion and struggle. This time, Benjamin Franklin said it best: "By failing to prepare, you are preparing to fail."

Food Groups

We know the major food groups: grains, vegetables, fruits, protein, and dairy. When deciding what to include in your diet, you'll want to consider the major nutrients that we all need. These are: carbohydrates, proteins, fats, vitamins, minerals, dietary fiber, and water.

So, what is in each food group, and what nutrients can you expect to find?

1. *Whole grains and starchy vegetables:*

   a. Whole grains, rather than refined grains, have a higher amount of carbohydrates, vitamins, and minerals. If you're looking for greater nutritional value, you can find whole grain in breads, cereals, pasta, rice, and oatmeal. Starchy vegetables like potatoes are in this group because they are similar to cooked grains, thanks to their macronutrient and calorie content. Brown rice and bulgur have their bran intact, and thus have more fiber, B vitamins, magnesium, and zinc. Other healthy grains are quinoa, oats, whole wheat pasta, farro, and barley. You can add these into your diet as side dishes, or on top of salads, and in soups.

2. *Fruits and non-starchy vegetables:*

   a. Rounding out meals and snacks with fresh vegetables and fruits is a great way to get the vitamins and fiber that you need. Opting for whole fruit instead of juice will increase your fiber intake. Canned goods that are reduced sodium and "no sugar added" fruits are ideal if you're worried about not being able to eat fresh produce fast enough. Canned goods are just as good when you're preparing salads and snacks. Always look to limit your sugar and salt intake in general. This can decrease the risk for health conditions like high blood pressure or heart disease. Fruits and vegetables are also rich in inflammation-fighting

antioxidants, vitamins, minerals, and fiber. It's recommended
we eat two cups of fruit and two-and-a-half to three cups of
vegetables every day.

3. Dairy and non-dairy alternatives:

a. Dairy provides essential calcium and vitamin D, and it's also
a good source of protein. Skim or one percent milk, calcium-
fortified soy foods, reduced-fat cheeses, and fat-free or low-fat
yogurt are healthy selections. Oat-based milks also offer the
calcium you're looking for.

4. Fish, poultry, meat, eggs, and alternatives:

a. Protein sources are essential for body repair, oxygenating your
blood cells, and even aiding digestion. Without proper protein,
fatigue is common, and some people may develop anemia after
a significant deprivation of this nutrient. Consuming a four-
ounce serving size of fish, meat, or poultry provides adequate
protein for most people. Eggs are also a good source of protein,
and they are economical. A serving of baked or broiled fish
is recommended twice a week as a source of heart-healthy
Omega-3 fat.

5. Fats

a. Food can be prepared with a variety of fats, butter, broth, and
oils. Butter is a tried-and-true favorite, especially in certain
cuisines, like in France. The ease of use, flavor, and flexibility
of butter makes it a wonderful starting point in cooking. Fats
help to absorb nutrients. Namely, vitamins A, D, E, and K.
If obesity and elevated cholesterol are dietary concerns for
you, then heart-healthy oils should be used. These are liquid
oils that contain essential fatty acids; an ideal complement to
cooked vegetables and salad.

b. There are two main categories to consider, polyunsaturated fat and monounsaturated fat. Polyunsaturated include Omega 6, which can be found in corn, safflower, sunflower, and soybean oils, and Omega 3 which can be found in cod liver oil, canola, flaxseed oil, salmon, sushi, anchovies, sardines, and walnuts. Monounsaturated fat is contained in olives, and canola and peanut oils.

Omega 6 and omega 3 fats work hand-in-hand for heart health. Aim to balance out the high levels of omega 6 fats in processed foods by adding back omega 3 fats and substituting monounsaturated fats for omega 6 in cooking.

To get the benefits of oil without consuming too many calories, always measure your oils when cooking. Dilute oils in dressings or sauces with water, vinegars, and citrus juices. Nuts, seeds, and dried fruit are rich sources of heart-healthy oils, protein, and fiber. A simple addition to salads, stir fries, or hot cereals if you really want to round out your meal.

The final piece of the puzzle we should consider is discretionary calories. Once you've eaten enough of the healthy foods described above, most people will choose foods or beverages that provide pleasure over nutrition. It becomes more of what you want, instead of what you need. In moderation, this is acceptable, and not something you should feel incredibly restrictive about. However, be careful not to indulge too heavily. And, if beer, wine, or spirits are your choice of discretionary calories, drink these responsibly!

Healthy Cooking Methods

Obviously, there are several different ways one can prepare a meal. Deciding to fry a cut of meat rather than roasting it will impact the nutritional value in different ways. Picking one over the other doesn't take a meal from healthy to unhealthy, but there are optimal ways to cook ingredients from the major food groups.

1. *Steaming*

a. Steaming is widely considered the healthiest way to cook vegetables, as it helps them retain the most nutrients. The Journal of Agriculture and Food Chemistry has shown that steaming carrots enhances their beta-carotene content, and steaming retains the most glucosinolates, the compounds in leafy greens like kale, brussels sprouts, and broccoli. These have been linked to helping prevent disease and cancer.

b. How to do it: Don't fret if you don't have a fancy appliance. Boil any appropriately sized pot of water, place a steam basket over the pot with the food you'd like to cook, and cover it with the lid. Steam for the recommended number of minutes, or until the vegetables become tender. Avoid oversteaming, as you likely won't want your vegetables to come out mushy. Steamed veggies always go great with a little added salt, spices, and olive oil. You can also use this method for seafood to maintain moistness.

2. *Stir-Frying*

a. Stir-frying is one of the best dry heat cooking methods to help clean out your fridge, and make use of all the proteins and fiber-rich veggies you have on hand. Plus, it gives you the opportunity to maximize the nutrition in your meals, adding a variety of vegetables with different flavors and textures. Stir-frying is intended to be a fairly rapid process that cooks food fast and makes vegetables more palatable. A great option if you're making a last-minute meal, no?

b. How to do it: Just heat a little bit of extra-virgin olive oil in a pan; it doesn't necessarily need to be a wok. Then, add the food you'd like to stir-fry and let the food sear until it tenderizes, stirring every 30 to 60 seconds. Season food with your choice of spices and herbs, sesame oil, soy sauce, peanut sauce, or a homemade sauce.

3. Roasting

a. Many vegetables and meats are amenable to roasting, a roast chicken, crunchy brussels sprouts, or crispy sweet potato wedges. The roasting process tenderizes meats and vegetables, thereby improving their texture and enhancing their flavor. For example, roasting butternut squash causes a caramelization that accentuates its sweetness to make it less bitter. When roasting, make sure to stick to a temperature that's below the oil's smoke point. Otherwise, you run the risk of burning things in the pan. The high heat used during roasting can diminish nutrients of the veggies, but you're still reaping their health-boosting benefits by including them, even if it's not the maximum amount.

b. How to do it: In a mixing bowl, combine the veggies you'd like to roast with a tablespoon of extra-virgin olive oil and your choice of seasonings. Stir until the ingredients are well-combined and the vegetables are well coated. Line a baking sheet with foil and lightly grease it. Then, spread the vegetable mixture evenly on the sheet pan and pop them in the oven. 350°F for about 45 minutes, or until they're lightly browned and crisp on the edges, will do the trick. Balsamic brussels sprouts and red grapes are elegant examples of this technique, and great for social events.

4. Poaching

a. Poaching is a novel and effective healthy cooking option for eggs, fruits, chicken, fish, or just about anything. This is a moist-heat cooking technique where food is submerged in water at a low temperature, usually between 140°F and 180°F, when white bubbles start forming around the edges.

b. How to do it: To perfectly poach an egg, fill a saucepan ⅔ full with water, a vegetable broth, or whatever liquid you're using. Bring the water to a boil, and then take it down to a low simmer. You'll see small bubbles come up to the surface and along the sides. Crack an egg into a ramekin or small cup. Carefully drop the egg into the water, then gently stir with a spatula, to ensure the egg doesn't stick to the pan. You can also add a dash of vinegar to the water, so the egg whites stay in a more compact shape. Allow the egg to poach for three to four minutes before removing it with a slotted spoon. Besides eggs, salmon or pears with red or white wine are good dishes to prepare using the poaching method.

5. Blanching

a. Blanching provides a cooking process to make vegetables crisp, yet tender. It's a good method for food preservation as well. For this technique, vegetables are submerged in a boiling pot of water for about seven minutes. Then, they are added to an ice bath. This maintains the vegetables' bright colors and helps retain their nutrients better than methods like steaming. The antioxidant activity in some veggies, such as beetroot, peppers, green beans, and spinach, can increase during the boiling process because the oxidative enzymes (which cause inflammation) are deactivated.

b. How to do it: Fill a large pot with water, add a tablespoon of sea salt and bring it to a boil. Add the vegetables to the pot and allow them to cook for a few minutes until their colors brighten. Then, immediately remove the veggies from the pot and run them under ice-cold water.

6. Grilling

a. Known to be a popular cooking method in the summer, grilling can be enjoyed year-round by using an indoor, cast-iron pan. Grill your favorite veggies over a stovetop in your home. The broiler in your oven is also great for this. Just prepare your food on a broiler pan and set it on your oven rack, between four and eight inches from the heat. Grilling helps remove excess fat from meat. It also gives vegetables and fruits a slightly smoky flavor.

b. How to do it: Trim the fat off the meat and wash the veggies. Make sure they're thoroughly dried before brushing them with vegetable or olive oil, then adding seasoning. Place the grill pan on the stovetop at a high-heat, until the pan is warmed up, then lower the heat to medium-low for three to four minutes. Flip the food on the pan to avoid drying them out, and cook for another three to four minutes. This is a tried-and-true method for vegetable skewers.

Think Outside of the Border

Some of the healthiest diets hail from Mediterranean and Asian cuisine, as these meals are rich in fresh, non-processed vegetables and grains. Spices, like curry powder, and herbs like basil, help flavor your food without adding salt. Thai and Greek salads are healthy, flavorful, and easy to prepare, often packed with ingredients across the major food groups.

Portion Control

Last on the list for healthy cooking, this is one of if not the most important aspects. Healthy foods, if piled on your plate or taking second and third portions, can be too much of a good thing. Moderation is what we should strive for with everything. Having an idea of healthy portions before serving yourself a meal can help you from eating more than you intended. And it will help you plan those trips to the grocery store in a more efficient, economical way!

CHAPTER 6

COOKING WITH WINE AND BEER

WINE

Wine is not only a popular beverage that accompanies meals, but a common ingredient in various dishes all over the world. Cookbooks and instructional videos are replete with recipes using wine to prepare food. The most common cooking wine is Pinot Grigio, followed by Cabernet Sauvignon. There are three main uses of wine in the kitchen, each with a specific function.

First off, it can be used as a marinade. Meat is bathed in your wine of choice and spices for several hours, which tenderizes it and adds complexity in flavor.

Wine can also serve as a cooking liquid. Like a marinade, this process enhances the meat's tenderness and flavor. However, unlike a marinade, this process uses heat to augment both the spices, and your cut of chicken, beef, pork, or even fish.

Lastly, wine can be added at the end of the cooking process, in a sauce or when basting to add flavor to a finished dish. All three of these methods will intensify and fortify the taste and aroma of the food and spices.

Choosing the Right Wine

Using the correct wine means selecting a wine that you enjoy drinking. Cooking will remove most of the alcohol, but the basic flavor will be present and even stronger due to evaporation of water. According to *The Guardian*, the age-old saying is true: if you wouldn't drink it, it's probably not going to taste that good when you put it in your food. So, be adventurous! Try more wines until you have a list of options that agree with your tastebuds. Then, find recipes that call for the types you gravitate towards.

Use Reasonably Priced Wine

There is little value in using high-end, pricey wine for cooking. You don't need to prepare a marinade that costs hundreds of dollars for you to put together. Reserve those wines for grand meals or special occasions, enjoyed alone in the appropriate glass.

Whichever cooking method you use, ingredients such as butter, olive oil, salt, and spices will always mix with the wine and change the flavor, compared to the slight tasting notes we find in a glass. The U.S. Department of Agriculture reports that 5 to 85 percent of residual alcohol will remain in the food, depending on the time when alcohol is added to the dish. If alcohol is added to boiling liquid and removed from the heat, then 85 percent of it will remain. In contrast, if alcohol is mixed into a dish that is baked or simmered, for two-and-a-half hours on average, then only five percent of the alcohol will remain.

If you're going to cook with wine, consider bottles between $8 to $20. If there is a $30 bottle you adore and you're really looking to splurge, we're sure your meal will taste amazing. Anything more isn't worth the expense.

Marinades

Marinades are widely used for meats, fish, and chicken. Cooking methods include simmering, roasting, and smoking. The advantage of using a great red or white wine is twofold; by adding acidity, you will further tenderize the meat, and the flavors of the wine marry with other ingredients to bring out the taste. An oak barrel red with peppery notes works well with black pepper and red meats, for example. You may also want to use a wine that complements the meat through converse flavors. A buttery, sweet piece of lobster pairs well with the tinny, bubbly qualities of a dry champagne. A yin-and-yang approach, if you will.

Always think of what wine you want to drink with the meal. Something like fish is better suited for a zesty, acidic white wine. A Pinot Gris or a Sauvignon Blanc. Marinating chicken with a white is also a reliable choice, but a creamy Chardonnay or a Burgundy (Bourgogne blanc) that offers hints of apple are a better fit. These are customary choices for Coq au Vin.

Red meat marinades will almost always call for red wines, typically Cabernet Sauvignon or Zinfandel, due to their robust flavors. Red wine also pairs well with dishes like these. An opportune time to open a more expensive bottle!

Time of Adding Wine

Describing the marinade process above notes that the wine is added before you start cooking. The only timing consideration is how long you're going to leave the meat to marinate. It's no secret that the longer you marinate the cut of meat, the stronger the flavor.

When cooking, the moment you add the wine depends on the dish you're preparing. However, a good rule of thumb across the board is not to add your wine too late. We recommend adding wine at least ten minutes before the end of the cooking process to let it properly cook down, burning off less-than-desirable flavors, and the pervasive alcohol taste.

In addition, when it comes to long-simmering stews, braises, or sauces, add your wine just after the liquid has started to simmer, or just after you've browned the meat and other ingredients. The wine will reduce some, which cooks off the alcohol and concentrate, leaving the delicious notes you're looking for. After that wine reduction, add other liquids such as stock or water.

Everyone has a different wine preference, but big, bold tannic reds will yield unwanted bitter flavors, as the tannins become more concentrated throughout the cooking process. So, while Cabernet Sauvignon is common, err on the cautious side and find ones that are more subtle. For some recipes, we think that Merlots or Pinot Noirs may be a better fit, as they aren't tannin-heavy, creating a smoother more balanced palate overall. Save your boldest wines for sipping.

Vermouth as a Wine Alternative

Vermouth is often used in cocktails such as martinis (dry vermouth) and manhattans (sweet vermouth). The perfect martini or manhattan calls for both! That said, these spirits can also be used for cooking. Vermouth is actually an aromatized, fortified wine that has additional alcohol added during the production process, containing herbs and spices that give it a more complex profile.

In this way, vermouth has more to offer than wine for certain dishes. Some people prefer cooking with vermouth as it's also more cost effective. The Auguste Escoffier School of Culinary Arts says that you can use dry vermouth in any dish that calls for white wine. It has a longer shelf life than an opened bottle of wine, too. Having some open at all times should not be an issue.

Our final tips for cooking with wine: avoid sweet wines. Most recipes call for wine to add acidity to the dish, not sweetness. Sweet wine will lack the characteristic bite, and sweet wine may cause a syrupy flavor for a meal that is supposed to be savory. Second tip? Sip wine while cooking and just enjoy the affair. Take your time to chop the vegetables, baste the meat, and select the herbs. Feel more connected to the food.

Our Favorite Recipes

CHICKEN PICCATA

Chicken piccata is a dish that uses white wine, butter, capers, chicken stock, olive oil, shallots or onions, and garlic. It is made with brisk timing, only taking about 30 minutes to cook after preparing the ingredients.

Ingredients;

- 2 lbs chicken boneless breasts o
- 1 cup dry white wine
- 2 tbsp olive oil
- 3 tbsp butter
- 1-2 shallots, medium chop
- 1 clove garlic
- ½ cups capers
- 3 tbsp flour
- 1 cup chicken stock
- 1 tsp Salt
- 1 tsp black pepper

Steps;

1. Season the chicken with 2 teaspoons salt and pepper on both sides. Place the flour on a plate. Dredge the chicken in the flour and shake off any excess. Discard the flour when finished dredging. The dredging phase is optional if carbohydrate dietary restrictions exist.

2. Heat 3 tablespoons butter and 2 tablespoons oil in a large skillet set over medium-high until the butter has melted.

3. Avoid crowding the pan and add ½ the chicken and sauté until golden brown, about 2½ - 3 minutes per side, until cooked through. This is best done in several batches and then set the chicken on a plate after cooking.

4. Add the shallot/onion to the pan drippings and sauté until soft and fragrant, about 1 minute and add garlic and sauté for 1 minute longer.

5. Add the stock and simmer until reduced by half, about 4-5 minutes.

6. Reduce heat to low, then stir in additional butter, capers, lemon juice, and white wine. Season with additional salt as needed. Some of the capers may be crushed to add more briny flavor. White wine used may be Chardonnay or Sauvignon Blanc.

7. Add the cooked chicken to the piccata sauce and simmer for another 10 minutes. Serve with pasta or salad.

COQ AU VIN

Coq au Vin is a French dish with the main ingredients being chicken, red wine, a large chopped onion, mushrooms, pearl onions, and bacon. Salt, pepper, thyme sprig, garlic, and bay leaf are used for seasoning. The traditional red wine used is a French Burgundy, but any good dry red wine is acceptable.

Ingredients;

- 1/2 cup thickly sliced bacon) cut into 1/4- by 1 1/2-inch strips
- 2 or more tablespoons olive oil
- 3 1/2 to 4 1/2 pounds chicken cut into parts, thoroughly dried
- 1/4 cup Cognac or Armagnac
- Salt and freshly ground black pepper

- 1 bay leaf
- 1/4 teaspoon dried thyme
- 20 pearl onions peeled
- 1 chopped onion
- 3 tablespoons all-purpose flour
- 2 cups red wine preferably Burgundy, Côtes du Rhône, or pinot noir
- 2 cups chicken or beef stock
- 1 garlic clove mashed or minced
- 1 tablespoon tomato paste
- 3/4 pound fresh mushrooms trimmed, rinsed, and quartered
- Fresh thyme sprigs for garnish (optional)

Steps;

1. Heat a Dutch oven or large pot enough to hold the chicken on medium-high heat. Add the bacon pieces and cook them until browned. Use a slotted spoon to remove the cooked bacon and set aside. Keep the bacon fat in the pan.

2. Add chopped onions and cook until translucent. Pat the chicken dry with paper towels and season all sides with salt and pepper. Working in batches if necessary, add the chicken, skin side down, to the hot pan. Brown the chicken well on all sides, about 10 minutes.

3. Add the pearl onions and garlic and cook a few minutes more. Spoon off any excess fat from the pot. Add the mushrooms. Add the chicken stock, wine, and herbs. Add back the bacon.

4. Lower heat to a simmer. Cover and cook for 20 to 25 minutes, or until chicken is tender and cooked through. (A thermometer inserted into the thickest part of the chicken should register at least 165°F.)

5. Remove the bay leaves, thyme sprigs, and garlic, and discard.

6. Boil quickly to reduce the liquid by three fourths until it becomes thick and saucy. Garnish with parsley and serve with potatoes or noodles.

BOEUF BOURGUIGNON

Boeuf Bourguignon (Beef Burgundy) is a French dish from the Burgundy region. This recipe calls for chunks of beef, beef broth, bacon, chopped onions and carrots, mushrooms, thyme, rosemary, and bay leaf. Beef Bourguignon *(pronounced "bef bur-gee-nyon,")* is stewed beef and the difference between this recipe and a regular beef stew is the amount of wine added to the broth, giving it a deep flavor.

Burgundy wine is often used, but a dry red wine such as Merlot, Cabernet Sauvignon, or Pinot Noir are acceptable.

Ingredients;

- 1 tablespoons extra-virgin olive oil
- 6 ounces (170g) bacon, roughly chopped
- 3 pounds (1 1/2 kg) beef brisket, trimmed of fat (chuck steak or stewing beef) cut into 2-inch chunks
- 1 large carrot sliced 1/2-inch thick
- 1 large white onion, diced
- 2 cloves garlic, minced (divided)
- 1 pinch coarse salt and freshly ground pepper
- 2 tablespoons flour
- 12 small pearl onions (optional)
- 3 cups red wine like Burgundy, Merlot, Pinot Noir
- 2-3 cups beef stock
- 2 tablespoons tomato paste
- 1 teaspoon fresh thyme, finely chopped
- 2 tablespoons fresh rosemary, finely chopped

- ◗ 2 bay leaves
- ◗ 1 pound fresh small white or brown mushrooms, quartered
- ◗ 2 tablespoons butter

Steps;

1. Preheat the oven to 325°F.

2. Cook bacon until crisp. Remove bacon from the pan, leaving the fat in the bottom of the pan.

3. Pat the beef dry with a paper towel and season with salt and pepper. Brown it in bacon fat in small batches over medium-high heat. Remove from the pan and set aside.

4. Add onions and carrots to the pan and cook for 2-3 minutes or just until the onion begins to soften. Add beef back to the pan, stir in flour, and cook for 2-3 minutes.

5. Add broth, wine, mushrooms, potatoes (if using), tomato paste, garlic, thyme, rosemary, and bay leaf. Cover and bake 2 ½ to 3 hours, until beef is tender.

6. Remove bay leaf, stir in bacon, and serve with potatoes.

BEER

Cooking with beer is a practice that almost certainly boasts as long a pedigree as cooking with wine. Beer delivers deep, earthy flavors to savory dishes like chili, soup, and stew; and a nutty, caramelized flavor to baked goods. It's great for just about every cooking technique, including braising, deglazing, battering, baking, sauce making, marinades, and simmering.

Any beer type can find its way into your kitchen, with different types offering a number of unique qualities. The hops used in brewing beer make it bitter by nature. However, the malt found in beer provides just enough natural sweetness, balancing everything out perfectly. In addition, foods high in sugars, such as carrots, corn, and caramelized onions are complemented by this bitterness. Most cultures that consume beer have a handful of recipes that call for it as an ingredient. From the classic Irish Beef and Guinness stew, to beer-battered fish and Belgian Carbonnades Flamandes. It's in rich and creamy foods like beer cheese, fondue, and French onion soup (as an alternative to wine).

Belgium has a long history of using beer and has created an entire range of dishes dubbed, *cuisine à la bière*. Although it was based on enduring local traditions, cuisine à la bière became popular in 1955 when Belgian master chef Raoul Morleghem published, *La Cuisine au pays de Gambrinus* (Cooking in the country of Gambrinus). Gambrinus was a mythical German king, now celebrated as an icon of beer. He was first written about by German historian Johannes Aventinus. Today, many of Belgium's best restaurants feature beer-based dishes.

In 1840 in the United States, Ballantine's Brewery was founded in Newark, New Jersey. It was, at one point, the fourth largest brewery in the country. In the 1930s, it popularized the use of beer in American dishes.

Unsurprisingly, beer-based dishes are common on the menus of brewpubs around the world. Chefs at high-end restaurants, long used to cooking with wine, are now also looking to beer, interested in experimenting with new flavors and textures. Exciting news for those who like to spice things up at the dinner table.

As with wine, the alcohol in beer will flash off during cooking. Beers have less acidity than wine, and as previously noted, any bitterness comes from the hops instead. One might hesitate to cook with very tannic wine; a very hoppy beer can be similar in difficulty to work with. Hop bitterness can be diminished by cooking after undergoing at least 90 minutes of simmering or braising. But, when properly paced, cooking can concentrate many of a beer's flavors, which will, in turn, enhance the meal.

Our advice for wine is fitting for beer: don't use a beer that you don't wish to drink.

Marinating

Many beers are the basis for a fine marinade to add flavor to meat and poultry. British brown ales and Belgian dubbels are great for beef, pork, and lamb; combined with shallots, herbs, salt, pepper, and garlic, these marinades are simple yet irresistible. If you desire, after the meat is removed, the marinade can be strained and used as a base for sauces.

Deglazing

After something has been sautéed or roasted in a pan or pot, concentrated, caramelized bits of the food remain stuck to the bottom of the cooking vessel. If you dissolve them by pouring beer into the still-hot pan, those caramelized flavors become an excellent basis for sauces. Use sweeter beers, like doppelbocks, if maltier, richer flavors are preferred. Acidic beers, such as gueuze, can work as well for a sour, citrus basis.

Beer Batter

Beer's carbonation adds lightness to batters, which you can use for fish, onion rings, or other breaded foods. Residual sugars from the beer also lends itself to a caramelized color, and a flavor that is more unique and creamier.

Stocks

Meat and vegetable stocks are the principal building blocks of many great cuisines. A variety of beers can replace water or wine when making stock. We recommend using lighter beers, like pale wheat beers and golden ales, to produce stocks for seafood and chicken dishes. And darker beers, such as Belgian dubbels and German dunkels, to produce stocks for meat dishes.

Stews and Casseroles

Beer can particularly shine in this regard, and carbonnade flamande, a beer-based beef and onion stew, is widely considered the national dish of Belgium. Long, slow simmering breaks down hop bitterness, leaving the beer's malt and fruit flavors intact.

Desserts

Imperial stouts can be used to make stout-flavored ice cream, or combined with ice cream to make floats. They can also be used in a wide assortment of cakes. Acidic beers, particularly gueuzes, make bracing and complex sorbets, while barley wines add an excellent kick to whipped cream.

Baking With Beer

1. Beer Bread is a classic quick bread where the beer, along with baking powder, provides natural yeast to help the loaf rise. Use a light lager unless you want a dark, bitter bread like Guinness Bread.
2. When baking with chocolate, reach for the darker stouts. The chocolate notes are brought out by the rich, dark beer.

Which Kind of Beer to Use

Akin to white and red wines, light and dark beers have distinctive flavor profiles, and understanding the differences is key to finding the best to add to a dish.

Here are our general guidelines for cooking with beer:

1. Wheat beers are great with chicken and seafood.

2. Ales, porters, and stouts are good with pork, beef, and lamb.

3. Belgian ales go great with hearty meat and game such as with Carbonnades Flamandes (see below).

4. Nut-brown ales pair well with stews and cheesy dishes.

5. Fruity beers are good choices for desserts, unless your recipe specifically calls for a particular beer.

Pale ale is a good choice because it is hoppy, rich, and fruity, without being overpowering. However, the ever-popular India Pale Ales (IPA's) may be a good standalone beer to drink but are often too bitter for cooking.

Our Favorite Recipes

CARBONNADES FLAMANDES

Carbonnades Flamandes is a Belgian beef stew made with hearty Belgian ale and plenty of onions. The flavor is a little sweet and sour, the sweet from the onions and either a little added sugar or tomato paste and the sour from a touch of mustard or vinegar.

Ingredients;

- 1 chuck roast
- 1 tsp Salt
- 1 tsp Ground black pepper

- 4 tbsp Butter
- 3 Yellow onions
- 3 tbsp Flour
- 1 cup Chicken or beef broth
- 12 ounces of Belgian beer
- 1 tsp dry Thyme
- 1 Bay leaf
- 1 tbsp Whole grain mustard
- ½ cup Brown sugar

Steps;

1. Cut the roast into 1-inch pieces. Pat the beef dry with paper towels, then season well with salt and pepper.

2. On the stovetop, heat 2 tablespoons of butter in a large, heavy-bottomed Dutch oven over medium-high heat. Working in batches, brown the meat, without stirring, about 3 minutes on each side (give the meat an opportunity to brown well). Add the remaining 2 tablespoons butter to the Dutch oven; reduce heat to medium.

3. Slice the onions 1/4 inch thick then add them and 1/2 teaspoon of salt to the Dutch oven. Cook for 15 minutes, or until the onions are browned.

4. Add the flour and stir for about 2 minutes, until the onions are evenly coated and the flour is lightly browned.

5. Stir in the broth and scrape the bottom of the Dutch oven to loosen any bits that have stuck to the bottom. Then, stir in the beer, thyme, bay leaf, brown sugar, browned beef with any of the accumulated juices, and salt and pepper to taste.

6. Increase heat to medium-high and bring to a full simmer. Reduce heat to low, partially cover, then let cook for 2 to 3 hours, until the beef is fork tender (alternatively, you can cook in the oven at 300°F). Stir occasionally, scraping up anything that is sticking

to the bottom of the pan. About 30 minutes before it finishes cooking, add the mustard and brown sugar.

7. Discard thyme and bay leaf. Adjust seasonings with salt and pepper to taste and serve.

8. Serve plain, with potatoes, over noodles, or with French fries.

BEER IN THE BRATS

Beer in the brats is a unique process that has been popularized in the past few years in the culinary arts and it promises to be impactful for beer and sausage lovers. It's an approach to cooking we are incredibly fond of.

Bratwurst or brats were originally brought to the U.S. by German immigrants, who would cook them much like Americans cook hot dogs today. It was in Milwaukee in 1954 that brats were introduced to the Milwaukee County Stadium during a baseball game that they really became popular. It is a well-known practice to boil brats in onions and beer and enjoy "beer brats" for outdoor events, picnics, and tailgating. However, it is less common to include beer into sausage or brats during the process of making the sausage.

The process of creating the "beer in the brats" has been recently created, and this unique method uses Sunshine Greetings beer from Central 28 Brewery in Debary, Florida. The first public tasting of this sausage occurred on October 23, 2021 at Petty's Meat Market in Longwood, Florida and prompted rave reviews of the sausage. The two versions of sausage were a spicy pork and a milder chicken. It also resulted in Central 28 Brewery selling out all their beer during that event.

CHAPTER 7

SPIRITUAL COOKING

Cooking with Spirits

We've discussed cooking with wine and beer; what about using spirits or liquors? Many of us have the old reliables in our liquor cabinet, like whiskey, bourbon, gin, vodka, and tequila. These are also the main ingredients in spirited recipes. The art and science of using alcohol in food is based on the physical properties of alcohol. It is a volatile but flavorful component of a recipe that can be mixed prior to cooking, during the process, or at the end with the flambé technique.

Alcohol works to improve flavors and aromas, even textures of food. Because it is polar (the molecule has one end that is polar and the other end is not) and a very volatile molecule, alcohol is able to interact with both fat and water soluble molecules in food, bringing fragrances to our senses more quickly.

Alcohol boils and converts to steam at 174°F (78° Celsius), while water boils at 212° F (100° Celsius). Simmering will cause part of the alcohol to evaporate faster than the water. Combining alcohol and water creates an azeotropic mixture, which means the water is hesitant to let go of the alcohol. Depending on cooking method and time, the alcohol is reduced by 60 to 90 percent. In addition, dilution plays a role in how much alcohol is in a dish. If a recipe requires ½ cup (4 ounces) of 100 proof alcohol to simmer in a sauce for 15 minutes, you're left with a little less than 1 ounce of alcohol. If the sauce serves four people, then you're down to a ¼ of an ounce per person. The proof is double the liquor's percentage of actual alcohol content, so those four ounces contain two ounces of alcohol.

Just enough for diners to enjoy the flavors, without the meal tasting too "boozy."

Vodka

Use in pasta sauces and pastries. Vodka is a neutral, mild accent that works like glue to help combine oil and water, ingredients that historically do not mix. In these instances, vodka serves to hold ingredients together, not to provide additional flavor.

It may also be used to combine cream and oil. For example, in pastas with rosa sauce (vodka, cream, tomato), vodka binds the cream and oil with the acidity from the tomatoes. This, in turn, brings out some extra flavor.

When baking desserts, like pie dough or pastries, adding a splash of vodka will prevent the ingredients from breaking down and separating. Vodka in small amounts with water and dry ingredients moistens dough and makes it easier to knead. The alcohol dries out, leaving no vodka flavor but prevents the dough from drying out.

Liqueurs

Typically used in fruit dishes, sweeter sauces, and desserts, liqueurs are distilled and flavored spirits which are very incredibly sweet. There are fruit, coffee, creme, flower, and even nut and herbal liqueurs. So, what's the best choice, and for which recipes?

Fruit liqueurs bring a light and refreshing bite to any beverage. Try adding a tablespoon or two of fruit-flavored liqueurs, like Aperol, Campari, or Cointreau, to sparkling water. You could also toss them into berries and other fruit salads to create a beautiful, syrupy coating. They also complement fillings for bundt cakes and parfaits.

Coffee and chocolate liqueurs, like Kahlua or Baileys, are richer and heavier on the tastebuds. These make great substitutes in baking for ingredients like vanilla, they can be stirred into hot fudge sauces, or may even be added as a splash in a cup of coffee.

Brandy and Cognac are both made from wines, meaning they are ideal for caramelizing in desserts or fruit dishes. You can also use them to soak into other sweets, like cakes, truffles, or creme brûlée, for extra richness.

Tequila

Tequila works great in vinaigrettes, marinades, and glazes for leaner proteins like fish or chicken. It provides a slight, fragrant kick that enhances flavor and thickens the texture of the sauce (similar to wine-based sauces). It has a natural smoky and citrus taste ideal in dishes that have a lot of citrus and acidity, as well as spice. Some of our pointers?

When incorporating blanco tequila, cook with dishes that have citrus elements, such as ceviche or a salad vinaigrette, as it's a light alcohol with floral notes.

Reposado tequila adds both smoky oak and vanilla flavors, as a result of the time it spends in oak barrels. A wonderful choice if you're looking for a kick in marinades and glazes. It also nicely accompanies vegetables on the grill.

Gin

Use gin in preserves, chutneys, and brines for richer proteins, like beef or pork. Gin is a combination of herbs and other natural flavors, also known as a botanica. It makes a perfect addition for both sweet and savory dishes:

Since gin's flavors are potent, it works really well in complex sauces, like chutneys, that are paired with stronger flavored meats, such as pork or dark-meat turkey.

This spirit also infuses a sweet, rich flavor in creamier desserts, like trifles and mousse. Gin's final application is in preserves, such as sweet jams or pickles, for that heavier floral, herbal taste.

Bourbon or Whiskey

Bourbon or whiskey work splendidly in sauces, desserts, and glazes for richer meats. Both spirits have sweet and smoky flavor profiles, like caramel. Like gin, they are delicious in either sweet or savory dishes. Next time you make bacon, try adding a maple-bourbon glaze! Our other tips are as follows:

Select a bourbon or whiskey you would drink, a similar approach when selecting a wine for the kitchen. If it doesn't taste good on its own, it won't in the dish either. Cook on low heat! Doing so and adding the alcohol away from an open flame will prevent a fire hazard.

Chicken takes well to tequila and rum, as does pork. But they also pair nicely with bourbon, even Scotch. For lamb, select a nice Scotch or Irish whiskey.

Brandy seems to work with almost everything, if used properly. Distilled wines such as Calvados (apple brandy), schnapps (various flavors), Cointreau, and Benedictine have applications in cooking as well. Kirshwasser is an integral part of fondue, as it lowers the melting point of the cheese, producing a smoother mixture.

Flambé with Liquor

Flambé (french for flaming) is the act of adding liquor to sauce and then igniting it, which cooks out the alcohol to create intensified flavor. This is a good way to impress your dinner guests. The best alcohols for flambé are darker-colored varieties such as brandy, cognac, and rum.

Our Favorite Recipes

Bourbon Pecan Pie is a year-round favorite, especially in the fall around the holidays. Bourbon is made with corn, barley, and rye (or wheat) in varying concentrations. It is then aged in oak barrels that add sugar to the liquid from the wood, itself. When used in cooking, it is the flavor of these components that come together to form a delightful combination. Because of its volatility, the bourbon evaporates, and the alcohol and water in the bourbon escape, leaving behind only the flavor of bourbon. The goal is about the flavor, not the alcohol.

Ingredients;

- 12 ounces toasted pecan halves, divided
- 4 large eggs, room temperature
- ½ cup packed dark brown sugar
- ¼ cup sugar
- 1 cup dark corn syrup
- 8 tablespoons unsalted butter, melted
- ¼ cup bourbon
- 2 teaspoons vanilla extract
- ¼ teaspoon salt
- 1 sheet refrigerated pie crust
- Vanilla ice cream (optional)

Steps;

1. Cut half the pecans until coarsely chopped. Combine eggs and sugars until well mixed. Add bourbon, corn syrup, butter, vanilla extract, salt, and chopped pecans.

2. Unroll the crust into a 9-inch metal pie plate and pour filling into crust. Arrange the remainder of pecan halves over filling. Place the filled pie in the freezer for 30 minutes.

3. Preheat oven to 425°. Bake until the crust is set, about 15 minutes. Reduce oven setting to 350°; continue baking until pie is puffed and set in the middle, about 1 hour (tent loosely with foil if needed to prevent overbrowning).

4. Cool. If desired, serve with vanilla ice cream.

Vodka And Tomato Pasta Sauce is a standard in many Italian restaurants and the combination of ingredients optimizes the sauce. Tomato is soluble in alcohol, and the combination with vodka does enhance the flavor of this sauce, especially if using canned tomatoes or bland supermarket tomatoes. Though it's traditionally made using heavy cream in addition to the vodka, cream and cheese such as ricotta can be used.

Ingredients;

- 2 tablespoons olive oil
- 1 small carrot, small onion, and celery stalk (finely diced)
- 1 clove garlic, peeled and finely chopped
- 1 bay leaf
- 1 teaspoon each dry oregano and basil
- 1 15-ounce can of diced tomatoes
- 1 tablespoon anchovy paste
- 2 tablespoons tomato paste
- ¼ cup vodka
- ½ cup heavy cream
- Salt and pepper

Steps;

1. Heat olive oil over medium heat. Add carrot, celery, onion, garlic, bay leaf, Italian herbs, salt, and pepper. Cook, stirring occasionally, until onion is translucent, about 10 minutes.

2. Add tomatoes, anchovy paste, and tomato paste and simmer, partially covered, for 45 minutes, stirring occasionally.

3. Add vodka and cream and simmer for another 15 minutes. Remove bay leaf and purée in a blender; taste and adjust seasonings.

4. Serve with shrimp sautéed in olive oil, garlic, pancetta, and Italian herbs over any pasta.

GEORGE'S BANANAS FOSTER

George's Bananas Foster is a classic dessert that combines bananas and vanilla ice cream with a rich sauce of butter, brown sugar, cinnamon, and dark rum. This recipe calls for flambé as a technique. After the alcohol burns off, the remaining sauce is infused with a roasted banana and caramel aroma.

Ingredients;

- ¼ cup butter
- ⅔ cup dark brown sugar
- 3 ½ tablespoons rum
- 1 teaspoon vanilla extract
- ½ teaspoon ground cinnamon
- ½ teaspoon nutmeg
- 3 bananas, peeled and sliced lengthwise and crosswise
- ¼ cup coarsely chopped walnuts

Steps;

1. Melt butter in a large, deep skillet over medium heat.
2. Stir in brown sugar, rum, vanilla, and cinnamon; bring to a low boil.
3. Place bananas and walnuts in the pan. Cook until bananas have softened, 1 to 2 minutes.
4. Serve at once over vanilla ice cream.

Roast Beef Tenderloin with cognac butter allows cognac's nutty and caramel notes to combine with butter, shallots, and thyme before melting over slices of tender beef.

Ingredients;

Cognac Butter

- 1 ½ tsp butter
- 3 tbsp minced shallots
- 3 tbsp cognac or brandy
- 6 ½ tbsp soft butter
- Salt, pepper, and thyme

Tenderloin

- 2 pounds beef tenderloin
- 1 tbsp Dijon mustard
- 1 tsp soy sauce
- Salt and pepper

Steps;

1. To prepare cognac butter, melt 1 ½ teaspoons butter in a small, nonstick skillet over medium-low heat. Add shallots; cook 2 minutes or until tender, stirring shallots occasionally. Carefully stir in cognac; cook 1 minute or until liquid is reduced by about one-third. Remove from heat; cool.

2. Place 6 ½ tablespoons butter in a small bowl; stir in cooled cognac mixture, 1 tablespoon thyme leaves, and ⅛ teaspoon black pepper. Cover and chill for 10 minutes. Divide butter mixture in half. Scrape each half of butter mixture onto a piece of plastic wrap; shape each portion into a 4-inch-long log. Wrap each butter log in plastic wrap; refrigerate or freeze 1 log for another use.

3. Preheat the oven to 425°.

4. To prepare tenderloin, combine mustard, salt, and pepper, and stir with a whisk. Spread mustard mixture over all sides of tenderloin; sprinkle with 2 tablespoons of thyme. Place tenderloin in a shallow roasting pan coated with cooking spray. Bake at 425° for 38 minutes or until a thermometer inserted in the center of tenderloin registers 135° or until desired degree of doneness. Let stand for 15 minutes.

5. Cut tenderloin crosswise into 16 slices. Arrange 2 slices on each of 8 plates. Cut 1 butter log into 8 slices; top each serving with 1 butter slice.

MINCE PIE

Mince pie (also Mincemeat pie in the United States, and Fruit Mince Pie in Australia and New Zealand) is a sweet pie of English origin filled with mincemeat, being a mixture of fruit, spices, and meat or animal fat. The pies are traditionally served during the holiday season. Mincemeat pie was brought to New England by English settlers in the 17th century. Originally a Christmas pie in Britain, mince pie has become a tradition during Thanksgiving. The ingredients for New England mincemeat pie are similar to the British one, with a mixture of apples, raisins, spices, and minced beef serving as the filling.

Ingredients;

- 15 oz canned pumpkin
- 9 oz evaporated milk
- ½ cup granulated sugar
- ½ cup brown sugar
- 2 eggs
- 1 tsp pumpkin spice

- 9-inch pie shell
- One jar mince meat
- 3 oz rum, cognac, whiskey (cinnamon whiskey works well)

Steps;

1. Preheat oven to 375 degrees. Whisk eggs and add remainder of ingredients and pour into pie shell.
2. Bake for 50 minutes until toothpick comes out clean.
3. Cool and refrigerate 3 hours and serve chilled.

COGNAC DUCK STEW

Cognac Duck Stew is similar to the famous French dish, pressed duck, however, this is a heartier, stewed version. Preparing this meal is a slow, yet rewarding process. Great for a dinner party, or the holiday season.

Ingredients;

- 6 duck legs or breasts or combination
- 12 small potatoes
- 20 small carrots
- One bag small onions
- One yellow onion
- One celery branch
- 3 oz cognac
- 2 cloves and 2 bay leafs
- 1 tbsp sugar
- 4 tbsp coarse salt
- A pinch cinnamon

Steps;

1. The night before, mix salt and duck legs in a large plastic bag overnight in the fridge. Drain.

2. Sear duck pieces in a frying pan over low heat, skin under: it must lose its fat and become very thin. Drain. Heat the duck in a Dutch oven with 2 quarts of hot water, leek, celery and onions, bay leaves, and cloves, and simmer for 1 - 2 hours.

3. An hour before serving, add carrots, turnips, potatoes with skin, pepper, and simmer for 45 minutes. Put the baby onions in a saucepan over low heat with 3 oz of water, salt, cinnamon, and sugar. When there is no more juice, remove fire.

4. To serve, cut onion into rings and place on a warm serving dish. Drain vegetables and thighs and place on top of onion rings. Pour the cognac into the broth, cook for 1 minute and pour the broth over the duck and vegetables.

CHAPTER 8

INFUSED FOODS

I nfusion is a method using dried herbs, flowers, or berries (sometimes referred to as botanicals) that easily release their active ingredients in water, oil, or alcohol.

In this process, a liquid is brought to an appropriate temperature, like boiling, and poured over the herb. The mixture then steeps in the liquid. These botanicals are removed through straining, which leaves an infusion. A prime example of this method is making tea, which dates back to the 10th century BC. Today, tea, coffee, herbal remedies, flavored oils, marinades, and more recently cannabis, are various things that are created using infusion as a method. This is even a technique used when preparing spa water or baths.

The amount of time the herbs are left in the liquid depends on the kind of infusion. This can range from seconds (for some kinds of Chinese tea) to hours, days, or even months (for marinating fruit in various types of alcohol).

- Black tea, chamomile, ginger, or lemon typically require metal steepers or strainers. Paper tea bags are the most commonly used tool for steeping, while preventing residual leaves from collecting at the bottom of each cup.

- Coffee can be made through percolation, where the liquid slowly passes through a filter or porous material. However, another means of infusion uses a French press (invented in 1929) which helps you manually brew a cup of coffee by straining the beans.

- ☛ Herbal remedies are commonly produced through infusions in water or oils. Flavored oils use edible oils or vinegar, infused with chilis, garlic, or lemon.

- ☛ Spa water can be a mix of cucumber and citrus slices, and herbs like mint. It has many potential health benefits, including weight loss, lowering blood pressure, helping bone health, and improving skin health. These ingredients can serve for relaxation in a bath or can be added to glass of water for a very hydrating drink.

Marinades

The goal of marinades is to enhance the flavor of an ingredient, tenderize meat, and/or preserve meat for the short term. The main forms of marinade are dry rubs, wet rubs (paste), and wet marinades. Amongst wet marinades are three types: acidic, enzyme, and dairy.

Dry Rubs

Commonly used for barbeque and grilling, dry rubs are applied prior to cooking. They tend to be made of salts, dried herbs, and spices, and are used to break down proteins while pulling other flavors in. Salt may draw out the meat's juices, but the enhanced flavor and texture of the meat contrast this, so it isn't tough to chew. Popular dry rub styles include barbeque, Cajun, Tex-Mex, and Jamaican.

Despite the recommendation to avoid using salt in marinades, they were historically always made of brine and even seawater was used. Marinade is derived from marinara, which in Latin and Italian means from, or, of the sea.

Wet Rubs (Pastes)

This category includes pesto (for poultry and seafood), jerk seasoning, and berbere spice paste. Pastes use a similar method to dry rubs but are mixed together with oil, alcohol, water, or other liquids.

Wet Marinades

Wet marinating requires immersing the meat in liquid. You want to avoid using too much salt; as previously stated, it draws out juices and may cause the meat to become tough. Cubed meat tends to absorb more flavor than full cuts because of the divided surface area.

What are the three types of wet marinades?

Acidic Marinades

Acidic marinades such as tomato juice, wine, vinegar, and citrus loosen protein bonds in the meat, thereby tenderizing it. They also amplify the flavor.

Enzyme Marinades

Papain or bromelain are enzymes that break down muscle fiber. They can be found in fruits such as kiwi, papaya leaves or fruit, and pineapple. Natural juices in the meat flow out, while the wet marinade flows in. But, when you go to cook it, your wet marinade that was absorbed will evaporate, leaving the meat dry and tough.

Note that leaving meat in enzyme marinades for too long can make its texture mushy and spongy.

Dairy Marinades

Milk, buttermilk, and yogurt are mildly acidic and may be the most effective tenderizing approach. The calcium in the dairy activates enzymes already in the meat, in the same way that aging meat does, which then break down proteins on their own.

Different flavors of marinades fit for different foods. You wouldn't use a red-wine-based marinade for poultry or fish, and fruit flavorings wouldn't go with beef, at least not for most contemporary tastes. Red wine is great for beef and pork. Fruit flavorings (like lemon) work well with fish. Marinades with seafood, poultry, and veggies are really there to add flavor, not to tenderize. Thus, soaking times for these are far shorter, and these marinades tend to be less acidic.

Our Favorite Recipes

Buttermilk Grilled or Baked Chicken is great if you're looking for the meat to be juicy, tender, and flavorful. This recipe feeds four, but can easily be batched for a party or larger gathering.

Ingredients;

- 4 chicken drumsticks (bone-in and skin-on)
- 4 chicken thighs (bone-in and skin-on)
- 1 ½ cups buttermilk
- 1 tablespoon mustard powder
- 1 tablespoon hot sauce
- 2 teaspoons minced garlic
- 3 teaspoons paprika
- Kosher salt, for seasoning chicken
- Vegetable oil (for grill)
- ¼ cup chopped fresh parsley

Steps;

1. In a medium bowl, whisk buttermilk, mustard powder, sriracha, garlic, and paprika until smooth.

2. Place the chicken in a plastic freezer bag; pour the buttermilk mixture over the chicken. Seal bag and refrigerate for 2 hours, or overnight.

3. Preheat outdoor grill for direct grilling over medium heat, as well as an indirect grilling area on the grill, if possible. Remove chicken from marinade, shaking off excess marinade; discard marinade. Season chicken with salt.

4. Lightly oil grill grates. Transfer chicken to grill over direct heat and cook for 20 minutes or until internal temperature reaches 165 degrees F, turning occasionally. If chicken starts to flare up over direct heat, move to the indirect heat area of the grill and continue cooking until cooked through.

5. If using an oven baking method, then set the oven at 350 degrees and bake for 40 minutes or to reach an internal temperature of 165 degrees.

6. Transfer chicken to a serving platter. Sprinkle with parsley and serve with lemon wedges, if desired.

Fruit and Alcohol Infusion

Marinating whole or sliced fruit in alcohol, also known as macerating, is a quick way to elevate their flavors. Autumn is the season to make apples and brandy; peaches and rum are a delicious summer treat. Macerating fruit also extends their shelf life.

You can eat the fruit straight from the bowl or jar, spoon it over ice cream, layer it into a trifle, or pair it with rich meats like duck. Thin-skinned fruits, such as berries or peaches, will over-soften if they sit in alcohol for too long. Hardier fruits like figs will stand up longer.

Our Favorite Recipes

Pineapple Rum is the perfect ingredient for cocktails at the beach. Or a way to bring a piece of the beach to you. You can make pineapple rum from scratch to keep in your drink fridge.

Ingredients;

- 1 whole pineapple
- 1 qt of white rum

Steps;

1. Core and slice the pineapple, then add contents to a clean glass jar.
2. Top with one quart of white rum and seal with an airtight lid.
3. Store in a cool, dark place for at least 3 days, or up to a week. Strain into a measuring cup or glass bowl through a fine mesh sieve and discard pineapple; repeat straining as necessary to remove all pineapple.
4. Seal in a clean jar and store in a cool dry place.

Cranberry Orange Cinnamon Whiskey

Cranberry Orange Cinnamon Whiskey is festive, and great for the holidays. The tang of citrus with a dark whiskey, and cinnamon, makes for a sweet, caramel drink with a hint of bitterness.

Ingredients;

- 2 cinnamon sticks
- ½ cup fresh cranberries
- 1 orange, sliced into wedges (keep peel on)
- 1 qt whiskey

Steps;

1. Take cranberries, orange, and cinnamon sticks and add them to a clean glass jar. Top with whiskey and seal with an airtight lid.

2. Store in a cool, dark place for at least 3 days, or up to a week. Strain into a measuring cup or glass bowl through a fine mesh sieve and discard cranberries, oranges, and cinnamon.

3. Repeat straining as needed to remove sediment.

4. Seal in a clean jar and store in the pantry.

Cooking With Cannabis

Eastern

The earliest mention of cannabis-infused food is as far back as 2000 B.C. in India. *Bhang* – a cannabis infused drink made with yogurt, nuts, spices, and rose water - is known as one of the oldest cannabis traditions.

Cannabis jam or Majoun is another early type of edible, first created by the nomadic Berber tribes of North Africa around the 11th century. The traditional Majoun recipe calls for cannabis extract, datura seeds, honey, nuts, kif, and sometimes dates and figs.

Western

The first cannabis edible recipe in the United States appeared in 1954 in *The Alice B. Toklas Cookbook*, with a recipe called *Hashish Fudge*. Toklas's name, and her 'brownies,' became synonymous with cannabis throughout the 1960s counterculture.

In some U.S. states that have legalized cannabis, edibles have experienced a dramatic rise in sales. There are those who are concerned about the danger edibles pose to children and inexperienced cannabis consumers. Calls to poison control have increased since 2008 due to dogs ingesting edibles. In Canada, cannabis-infused food products were legalized in October 2018, but regulatory restrictions and reduced consumer interest may inhibit innovation.

A cannabis edible, also known as a cannabis-infused food or simply an edible, is a food product (either homemade or produced commercially) that contains cannabinoid acids, converted to their orally bioactive form from cannabis extract. Although *edible* may refer to either a food or a drink, a cannabis-infused drink may be referred to more specifically as a liquid edible or drinkable.

Unlike smoking, which passes rapidly into the bloodstream, peaking in about ten minutes and wearing off in a couple of hours, cannabis edibles may take hours to digest. Their effects may peak two to three hours after consumption and persist for around six hours. The food or drink used may affect both the timing and potency of the dose ingested.

Terpenes are the chemical compounds in cannabis that give it that characteristic funky smell and taste. This can make it a challenge to cook with, according to Portland cookbook author Laurie Wolf. She says the key when eating infused food is to be extremely patient in waiting for the effects to set in, lest you go on a trip you didn't mean to buy a ticket for: *"It can take two, it can even take three hours on occasion, depending on when you've eaten, what your metabolism is like."*

Most edibles contain a significant amount of THC, which can induce effects like: relaxation, sleepiness, dry mouth, depersonalization, increased anxiety, and even paranoia and hallucinations. THC-dominant edibles are consumed for recreational and medical purposes. Some edibles contain a negligible amount of THC and are instead dominant in other cannabinoids, most commonly cannabidiol (CBD). The main characteristic of cannabis edibles is that they take longer to affect users compared to smoked cannabis.

Foods and beverages made from non-psychoactive cannabis products are known as hemp foods. Jared "Roilty" Farina is a well-known chef in Colorado who has developed the art of cannabis and teaches his technique to other chefs around the world.

Below is our favorite Roilty recipe, and one we have used with great success.

Sticky-icky honey-glazed salmon and fresh veggies are sweet, and great for chefs who love the taste of garlic. It only takes twenty minutes to put together. It is best to prepare the proteins (salmon) last to avoid overcooking.

Ingredients;

For salmon

- 4 salmon filets (6 oz each)
- ½ teaspoon kosher salt
- ½ teaspoon black pepper
- ½ teaspoon paprika

For sauce

- 3 tablespoon butter
- 2 teaspoon olive oil
- 1 tablespoon Chef Roilty's infused olive oil
- 6 cloves garlic (minced)
- ½ cup honey
- 3 tablespoons water
- 3 tablespoons soy sauce
- 1 tablespoon sriracha sauce
- 2 tablespoons lemon juice (recommend fresh-squeezed)

Steps;

1. Use a 12" wide, oven-safe skillet with a lid, pat the filets dry, season on both sides, then set aside. Adjust oven rack to middle position and preheat to 'broil'.

2. Add butter and oil to skillet over mid-high heat. Once the butter has melted, add garlic, water, soy sauce, sriracha, honey, and lemon juice. Cook for 30 seconds.

3. Add salmon filets and cook for 3 minutes. While salmon cooks, use a spoon to baste the salmon frequently.

4. Broil salmon for about 5 minutes, basting just once more midway through.

5. Remove salmon from pan and set on cutting board to rest.

6. Reserve ½ cup of the remaining sauce from the pan and add 1 tablespoon of Chef Roilty infused olive oil. This will make the ½ cup of reserved sauce 100mg THC and easy to dose each dish accordingly.

Your salmon is ready once it looks browned (caramelized) and is slightly charred. An internal temperature of 145°F degrees is recommended.

Remaining cooking tips from Chef Roilty?

- While cooking, spooning sauce over your filets (basting) will keep the meat moist.

- Want to make it easier on yourself? Always sear skin-side first to lock in flavor and prevent the delicate flesh from sticking to your pan.

- You're better off slightly under-cooking your fish than over-cooking it.

☞ Garnish your dish with minced parsley to spruce up your presentation. Leftover salmon should be refrigerated in an airtight container and consumed within a couple of days.

85

CUTTING, CARVING AND COOKING FOR SUCCESS

Bavette

OBLIQUUS INTERNUS ABDOMINIS

Bavette is French translating to "Bib" for English, comes from lower chest, abdominal bottom sirloin or under belly of a bovine next to the Hanger and Flank. The muscle fibers are ridge-like and the grainy texture has a rich beefy taste similar to Flank yet has a more savory factor due to more marbling. We sometimes call this supercharged Flank steak. Also referred to as faux hanger, flap meat, flap steak, and sirloin steak tip.

THE CUT

Bavette typically comes in a long flat piece with silver skin accompanied by fat, trimming properly leaves for a nice long strip of meat about 2-3 feet long. Typically after trimming Bavette is cut into ⅓ of the actual size from a long piece. Can be eaten whole or cut into strips which make great fajitas.

HOW TO SLICE

Decipher the grain direction of the Bavette and begin to separate into sections, Slice sections against the grain.

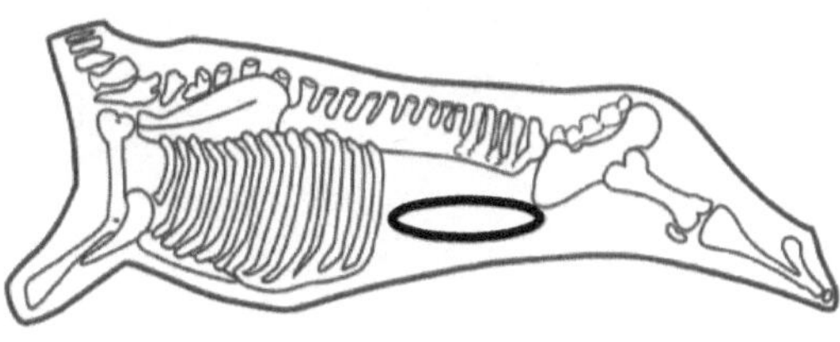

Bistro Filet
TERES MAJOR

Bistro filet comes from chuck primal located in the front shoulder clod teres major muscle of the bovine. Bistro filet is a more cost effective cut while a lot of people confuse it for real tenderloin, while very tender the texture and beefy taste are not comparable to filet mignon. Also referred to as a rat, shoulder tender, petite tender, filet mignon in disguise, and poor man's filet.

THE CUT

8 - 12 oz for each lean piece with minimal fat and silver skin seemed out for trimming.

HOW TO SLICE

Slice diagonally into medallion shaped pieces, sliced in strips for stir fry, and also cubed for kabob meat.

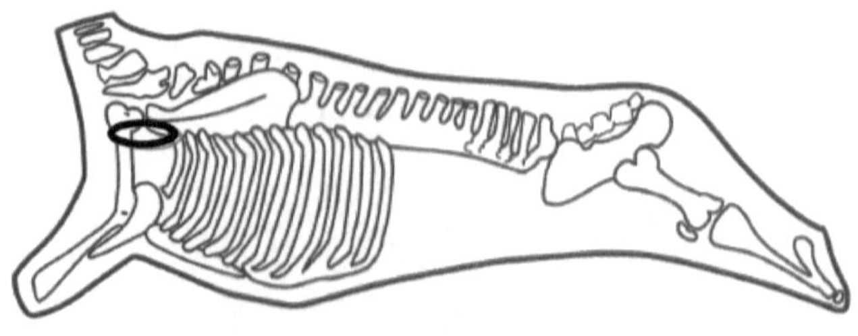

Boneless Sirloin

VASTUS LATERALIS/GLUTEOBICEPS/GLUTEUS MEDIUS/RECTUS FEMORIS

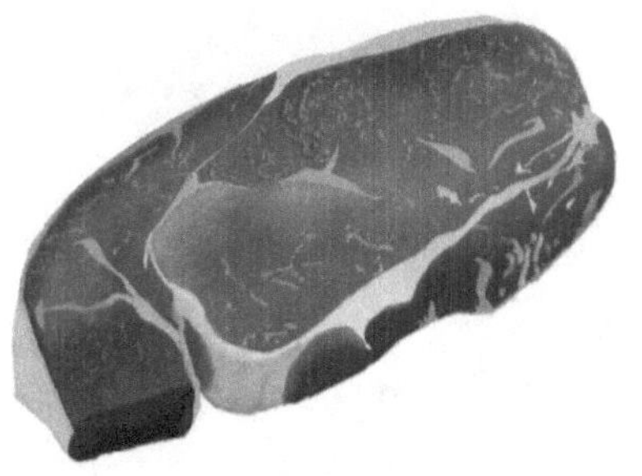

Boneless sirloin is one of the largest loin cuts derived from primal loin, this sub cut extends to several muscles. Top sirloin area is closest to the leg or rump. Boneless sirloin comes in a variety of size cuts depending on request. Firm tenderness texture with a beefy flavor. Also can be referred to as NY sirloin steak, butt steak, shell sirloin steak.

THE CUT

Start on a gristly side trimming fat and silver skin from the bottom layer. Leaving ¼ inch intermuscular cap cutting steaks 2-2 ½ inches thickness.

HOW TO SLICE

Decipher the grain direction of the steak and begin to separate into sections, Slice sections against the grain. Sliced into strips for stir fry and cubed for kabob meat.

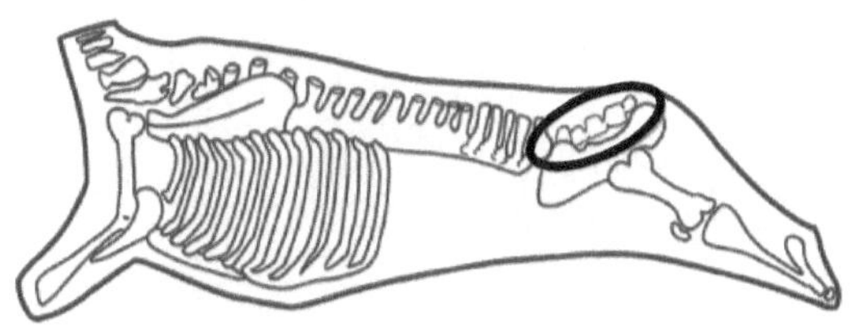

Brisket
PECTORALIS MAJOR/MINOR

Brisket is derived from the bovine breast or lower chest located in front of the foreshank below the chuck area. Brisket is divided into two sub cuts the pectoralis major is a leaner flatter more conformed cut called the "Flat end", while the pectoralis minor is a larger end being fattier called "Point end" or sometimes referred as "Deckle/Nose."

THE CUT

Brisket has a very large amount of fat marbled throughout the loin. Trimming the majority of the fat on top of meat is recommended for proper trimming of this large cut. Brisket early on was discarded, ground up, or used for stew meat.

HOW TO SLICE

Brisket is a tougher slice that needs to be braised or slow cooked to break down intramuscular fat to properly prepare. Slice the flat away from the point end, the grain changes between those sections. Decipher grain on both ends and cut against the grain.

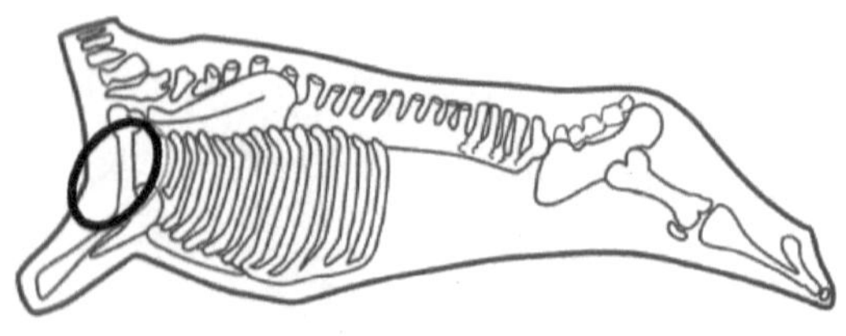

Chuck Roast

SERRATUS VENTRALIS/RHOMBOIDEUS THORACIS/ SEMISPINALIS THORACIS

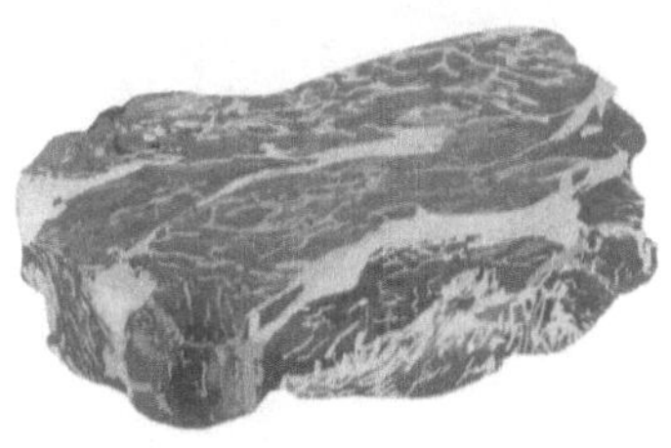

Chuck roast consists of multiple muscles derived from the area of neck, shoulder, upper arm location between shoulder blade and ribs of the bovine house the chuck roll. This is an economical cut that is utilized for slow or pressure cooking. Also referred to as America's beef roast and boneless chuck filet.

THE CUT

The boneless chuck roll will have the majority of intermuscular fat trimmed off along with silver skin before breaking into sub cuts 2 - 3 LBS.

HOW TO SLICE

Chuck roast area contains a high amount of connective tissues which can be tough if not prepared properly. Chuck roast has high amounts of collagen and marbling which can make the intense flavor of this cut when cooked down properly. Cooking low and slow will make the chuck roast breakdown and meat easy to pull apart.

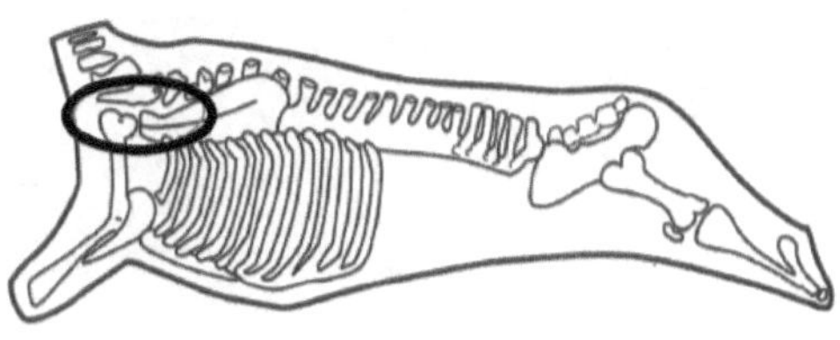

Delmonico
LONGISSIMUS/SPINALIS DORSI

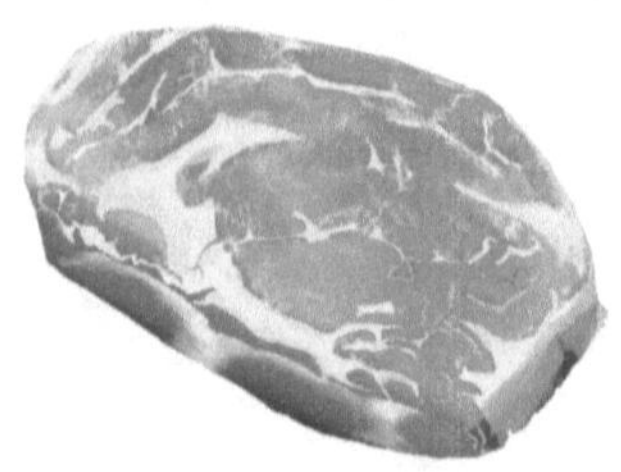

Delmonico is essentially a ribeye with the rib bone removed, The Delmonico originated from the mid 19th century by the Delmonico brothers in New York City. The Delmonico traditionally cut from the chuck eye roll the front rib end of the bovine. The Delmonico cut has intense intramuscular marbling with smooth beefy flavor and juiciness. Also referred to as beauty steak, boneless ribeye, chuck filet steak, English steak, scotch filet, and spencer steak.

THE CUT

Rib portion of ribeye is removed leaving just loin which can be cut into variations of thickness of steak typically 1 ¼ inches, majority of fat tip end trimmed off.

HOW TO SLICE

Delmonico can be sliced according to consumer, served as a whole cut typically or sliced into strips.

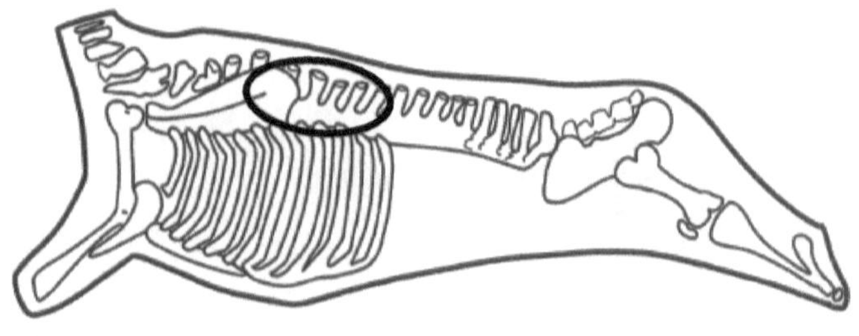

Eye Round
SEMITENDINOSUS

Fairly lean cut being derived from a hamstring muscle housed hind quarter of the leg in between the inside round and bottom round known as semitendinosus. Eye round is a cost effective roast but not top flavor as compared to higher cuts. Also referred to as round eye or pot roast.

THE CUT

Eye round is surrounded with fat and silver skin that should be seemed out leaving a long and cylindrical shaped roast.

HOW TO SLICE

This long circular shape cut which is tough when sliced into individual steaks suggests that it should be cooked as a roast. Slice thinly after preparation due to the meat texture being more firm. Also can slice into stew meat and run through cuber for cubed steak.

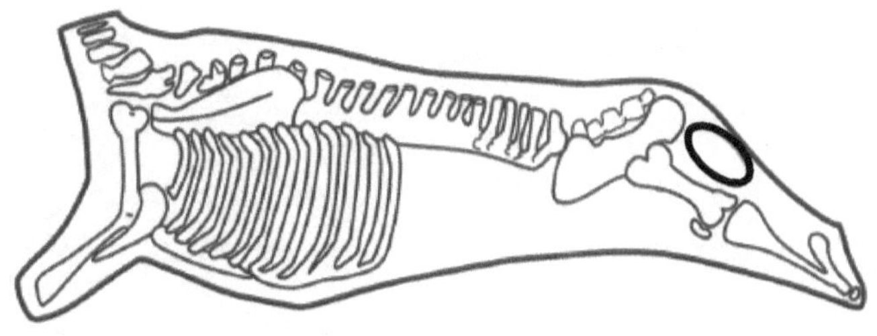

Filet Mignon
PSOAS MAJOR

Filet mignon is derived from the tenderloin area housed near the spine of the bovine known as the Psoas major muscle. Filet mignon is the superior of the cuts being the supreme of tenderness with ultimate buttery beef flavor this cut can be very pricey depending on its USDA grading. Filet mignon is French wording meaning "fine" or "tender" filet and also can be referred to as filet de boeuf.

THE CUT

Proper trimming will result in removing outer layers of fat, removing the majority of the chain of meaty fat, seeming out all silver skin by getting underneath tightly.

HOW TO SLICE

Tenderloin can be constructed into an entire loin roast or cut into individual cylindrical steaks about 1 ½ - 2 ½ inches lengthwise.

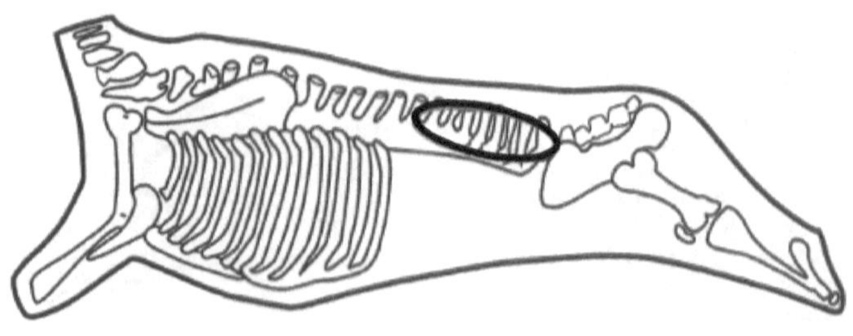

Flat iron
INFRASPINATUS

A tender composition cut with the grain from the frontal shoulder underneath the shoulder blade/top blade adjacent to the shoulder lengthwise atop the line of gristle. Its fascia or sinew is housed down the middle when properly cut is removed to present two filets, a method used to create the flat iron steak. Also referred to as butlers steak, oyster blade steak, top blade steak, top blade filet, and shoulder top blade steak.

THE CUT

Removing the fat and silver skin from the outside then carefully removing the sinew housed in between both filets. Working knife right down the middle to split filets and seem out excess sinew. Flat iron can be one of the most difficult cuts to execute properly.

HOW TO SLICE

Decipher direction of the grain and slice into small strips for tenderness.

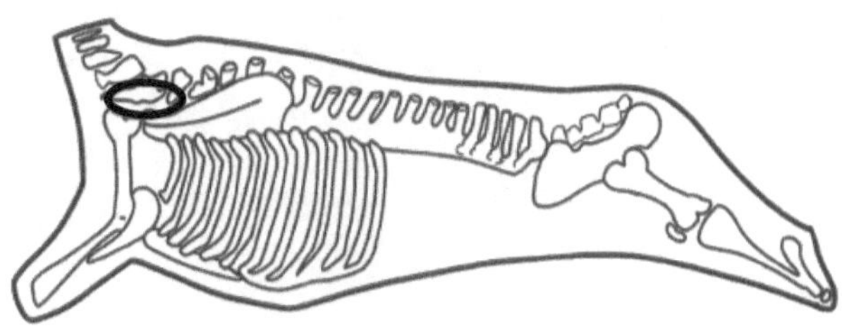

Flank
TRANSVERSUS ABDOMINUS

Flank steak is a lean flat cut muscle that comes from the lower area of the short loin underside the bovine, that contains long fiber muscles which make it tough. When prepared properly flank has a favorable delicious taste and texture that can be chewy normally enjoyed typically by Asian culture. Also referred to as a jiff or jiffy steak and in Colombia call "sobrebarriga" translated "Over the belly".

THE CUT

Flank can contain small amounts of fat and silver skin that should be seemed out to give a roundish shape.

HOW TO SLICE

Flank being sliced into small strips against the grain will provide tenderness.

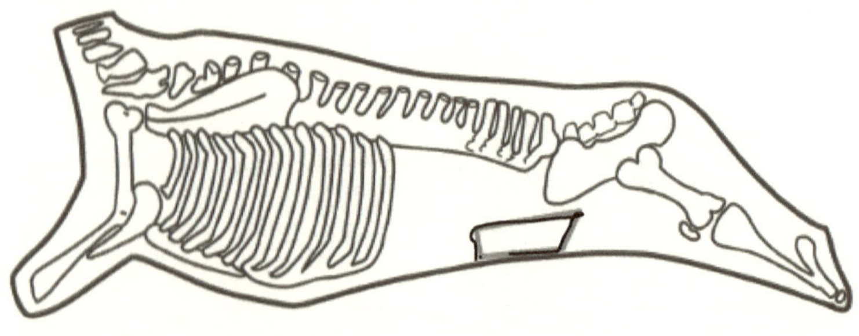

London Broil
ADDUCTOR/SEMIMEMBRANOSUS

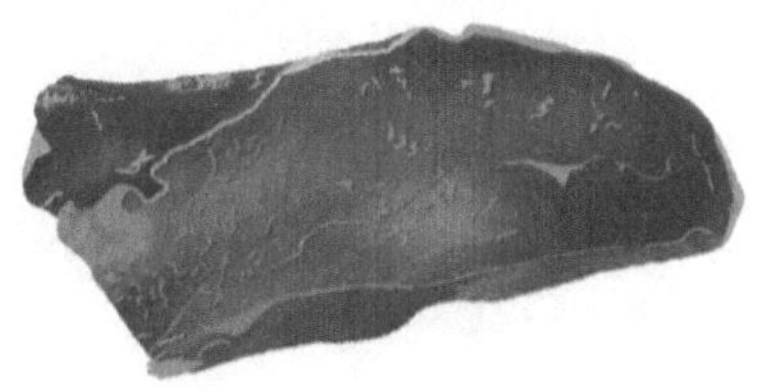

Inside round is a primal loin when broken down to sub cuts from adductor and semimembranosus muscles derive the London Broil. Inside round but also categorized as top round can be used for a variety of steaks. Inside round cut is typically used for a more economical standard of meat utilization, London broil being a more selected choice of supermarket meats. Also referred to as top round first cut and top round steak roast.

THE CUT

Inside round is surrounded by an ample amount of intramuscular fat and silver skin from the bottom and top of the loin. Fat and silver skin should be removed majority before breaking down into sub cuts. Post trimming this loin can be broken down into 2' inch thick steaks that can feed up to 4 people.

HOW TO SLICE

Most commonly used for this cut is London broil but also makes great jerky and Philly cheesesteak can weigh up to 15-20 LBS total. Slice against the grain for more tenderness.

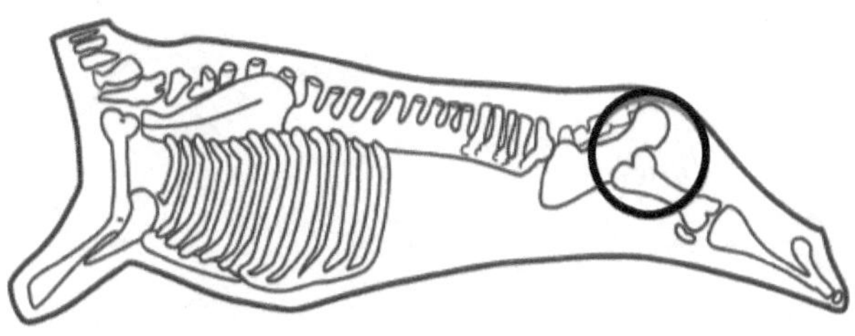

Hanger
CRURA/DIAPHRAGM

Hanger steak is a tender cut that is derived from the plate area of the crura/diaphragm muscle of the bovine. The name hanger comes from the fact that the cut of meat just "hangs" from the upper belly of the animal. Being one of the most tender cuts this is derived as a pair of muscles that form a chromosome looking shape that contains a long inedible connective tissue running down the center of both pieces of meat. Also referred to as the butchers cut, butchers steak, and hanging tenderloin.

THE CUT

When properly trimming the hanger should have all fat and silver skin removed from the surrounding cut. The middle of both cuts house a tough inedible sinew which must be seemed out for proper preparation of meat.

HOW TO SLICE

Slicing into chunked pieces against the grain will provide tenderness.

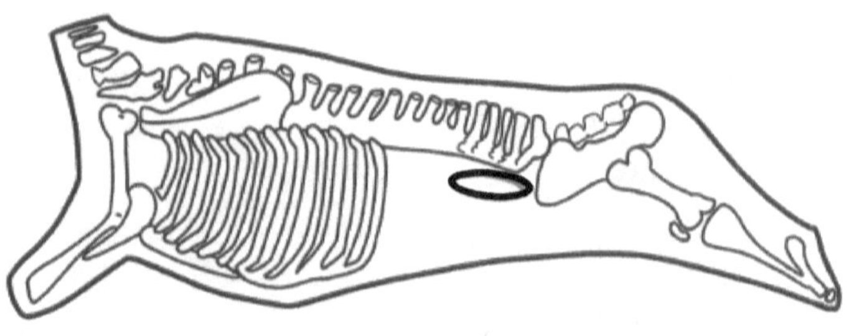

Oxtail
COCCYGEUS

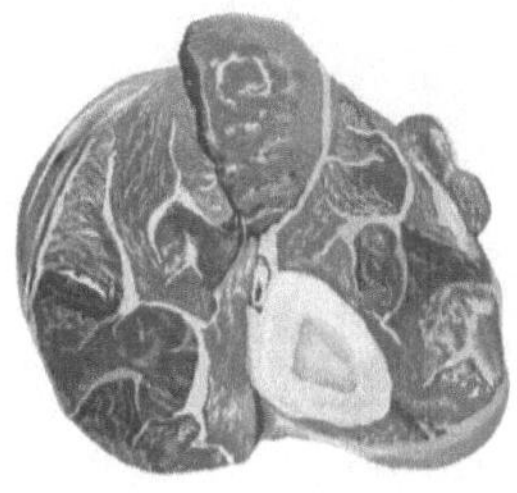

Oxtail is a refereed to the tail of an ox generally, now used for the culinary term for tail of bovine. Movement from the tail comes from pairs of coccygeal muscles while thicker cuts are derived closer to the bovine receding to the tail. Rich beef flavor that has a generous portion of marrow centered in the bone. Oxtail cut mostly has bone, minuscule amounts of meat, and can be very pricey.

THE CUT

This can be cut in between the bone where the cartilage is located. Normally produces a round piece about 2' inches with bone centered in the middle. Closer to the bovine the bigger diameter of meat can be procured.

HOW TO SLICE

Oxtail is normally cooked braised when preparing or can be cooked down into soup or stew.

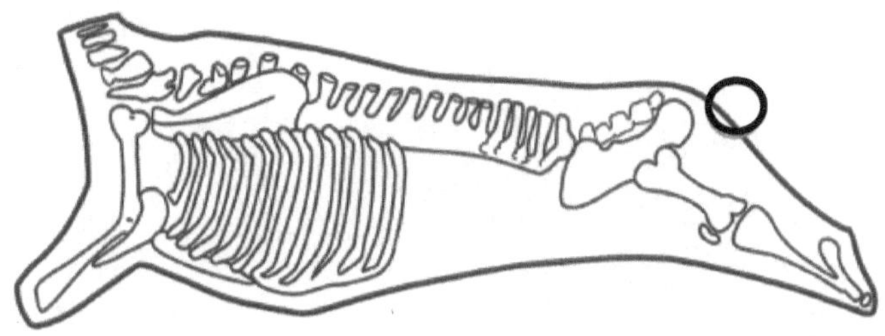

NY Strip

LONGISSIMUS DORSI

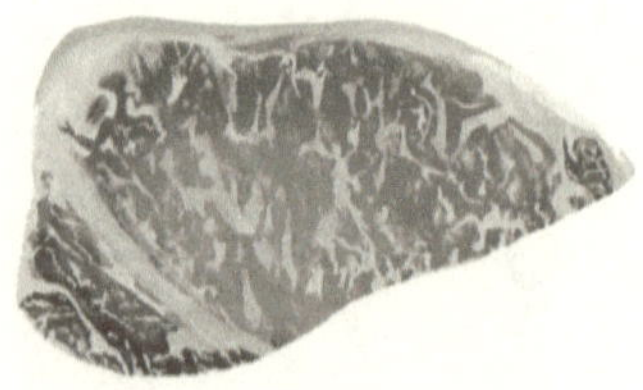

The main muscle derived from the NY strip is the longissimus dorsi extended hip trailing up to the shoulder blade, same muscle rib-eye steak. The name Boneless strip comes from the fact that the cut is literally "stripped" from the short loin of bovine. NY Strips are a staple across steakhouses and a carnivore's top choice when ordering steak. NY strip is median cost cut widely chosen boneless and also comes bone-in. NY strip being so widely sought out it shares many referred names like ambassador steak, boneless club steak, Kansas City strip, and Texas strip.

THE CUT

Edging off where you intend to make the first cut, making each piece at least 1 ¼ inches thickness. Trimming the connective tissue at front butt end along with outer intermuscular fat.

HOW TO SLICE

If you prefer a well done steak go with the sirloin end of the short loin, medium to rare side go with the rib end. Decipher grain and slice against into thin strips.

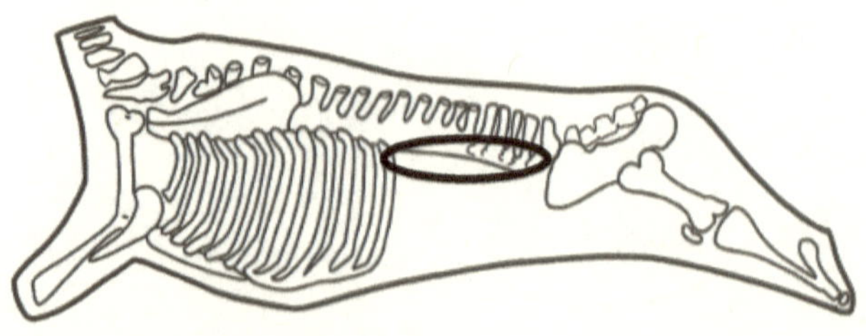

Porterhouse

LONGISSIMUS DORSI/PSOAS MAJOR

The Porterhouse is derived from the bone in short loin where the lumbar vertebra is shaped like a "T" and Longissimus dorsi (strip loin) adjacent to the Psoas Major (Tenderloin). The difference between the Porterhouse and T-bone is that the Porterhouse is taken further back of short loin containing a larger cut of the Psoas Major while the T-bone has a minuscule amount of Psoas Major. Normal guidelines from the USDA suggest 1 ¼ Inches to be categorized as a Porterhouse steak. Also referred as a king steak.

THE CUT

Bone saw individual steaks at least 1 ¼ inch followed by bone dusting off each sub cut. Removing intermuscular fat surrounding the short loin can be done before or after individual steaks are cut.

HOW TO SLICE

Remove filet and strip from the bone after preparation, slice against the grain for tenderness.

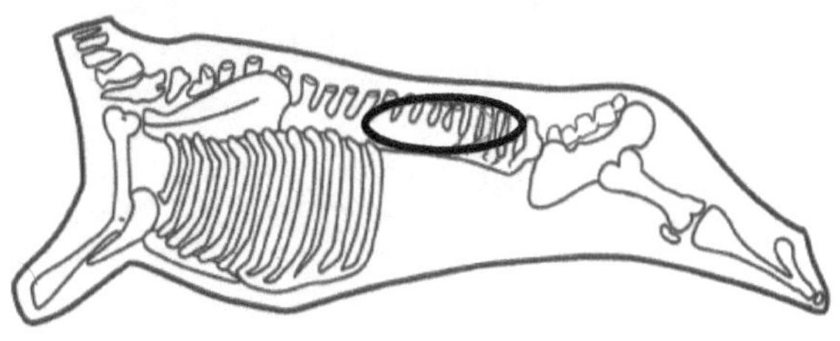

Picanha
BICEP FEMORIS

Picanha is a triangular shaped piece found on the top butt/ rump area muscle known as bicep femoris. It is a cut that started popularity in Brazil becoming more popular on the west coast steakhouses of America. If prepared properly it serves as a tender cut with well marbling. Also can be referred as coulette (French) sirloin cap, rump cap, and rump hood.

THE CUT

Trimming the fat and silver skin away from the meat side of the cap leaves a triangular shaped roast. Fat cap should have at least ¼' inch remaining on it.

HOW TO SLICE

Decipher direction of the grain and slice against it, commonly into 1' inch thickness.

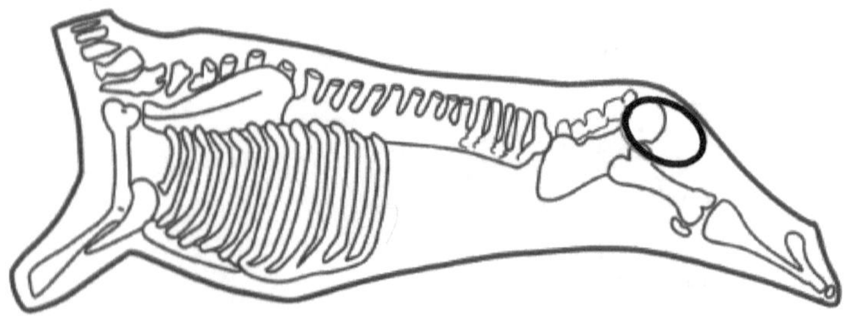

Rump Roast
GASTROCNEMIUS

Rump roast taken from bottom round or outside round is a huge piece more commonly used for roasts can and weigh up to 15 LBS. This cut is tough and should be cooked at a slow rate. It also can be utilized to use grinds for lean types of ground beef.

THE CUT

The large loin can be broken down into smaller cuts used for roasts, this typically can vary depending on the size of roast required.

HOW TO SLICE

After cooking rump roast it should be sliced very thin to avoid any type of toughness this specific meat can normally have.

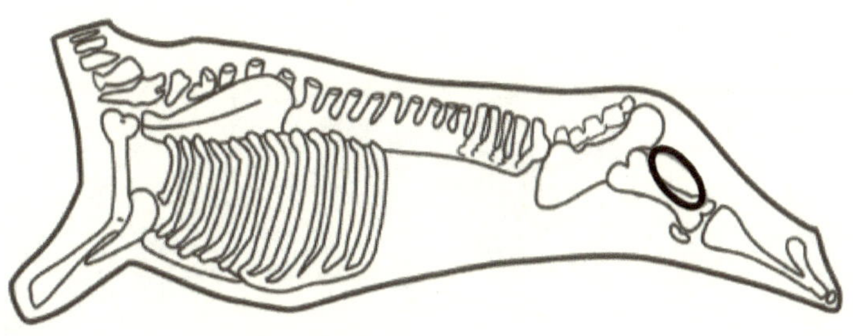

Ribeye

LONGISSIMUS/SPINALIS DORSI

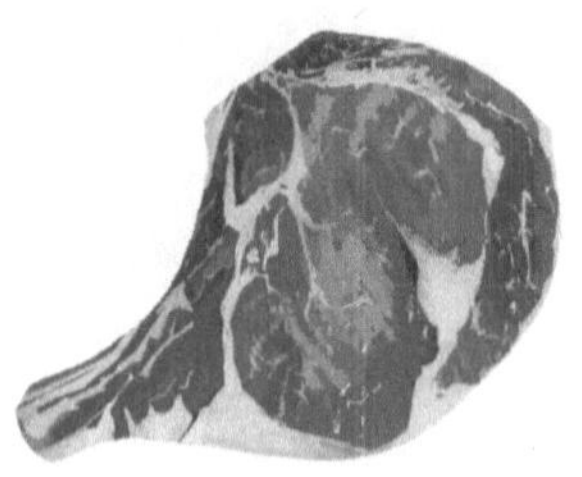

Bone in rib-eye is traditionally cut from the upper rib primal that stretches through 13 individual ribs, normally cut starting at the sixth rib and ending with the twelfth. The Longissimus dorsi is translated as "eye of rib-eye".

THE CUT

Removing intermuscular fat surrounding the beef rib primal loin prior to bone sawing individually into at least 1 ¼ inch thickness, followed by bone dusting each piece cut.

HOW TO SLICE

Remove bone after preparation of steak. Decipher the grain direction and slice against the grain for tenderness.

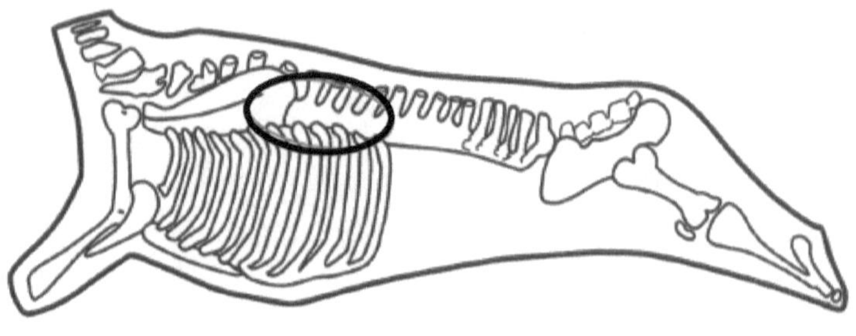

Skirt

TRANSVERSUS ABDOMINIS

Skirt steak comes from 2 different locations from the bovine: inside skirt and outside skirt are long flat pieces of meat. Outside is the more popular and obtainable used cut derived under the diaphragm muscle. Outside skirt is not as wide as the inside skirt, yet is much more tender. Inside skirt muscle Transversus Abdominis is located deeper within the inner walls of the bovine's chest closer to the lungs. Also referred to as fajita steak, Philadelphia steak, and Romanian steak.

THE CUT

Skirt steak contains a fair amount of connective tissue and fat surrounding meat being removed majority to experience tender results of cut. Outside Skirt - 2-4 Inches in diameter and ½-1 Inch thick. Inside Skirt - 4-6 Inches in diameter and ¼-¾ Inch thick

HOW TO SLICE

Slice into 3 inch sections to separate steak after preparation, slice into thin strips against the grain for tenderness.

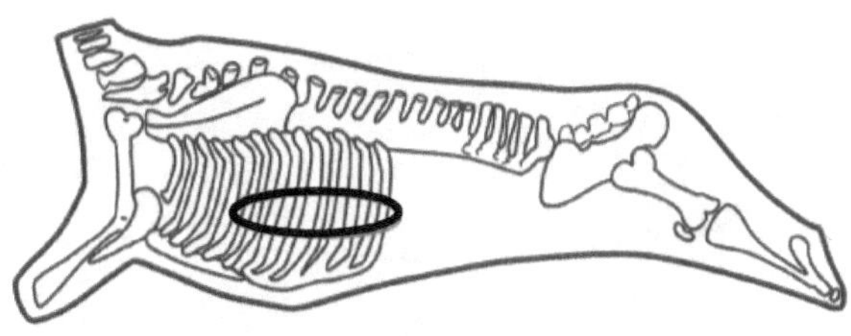

Short Ribs
SERRATUS VENTRALIS

Short ribs are derived from the belly area behind the brisket and lower part of the beef plate rib or Serratus Ventralis muscle. Short ribs can be cut into 2 main varieties, English and Flanken style. English style ribs are cut along the bone parallel rectangle sort shape after being derived from plate. Flanken style are cut horizontally across the 3 ribs section to give the look of laddering of 3 bones in the middle.

THE CUT

English style is cut along the bone being about 2 ½ - 4 INCHES long. Flanken style are cut crosswise from the plate with a bone saw 1 ½ - 2 INCHES thick.

HOW TO SLICE

English style the ribs are cut along the bone with the bone normally used for slow cooking or braising. Flanken style are cut across the 3 ribs section of the plate.

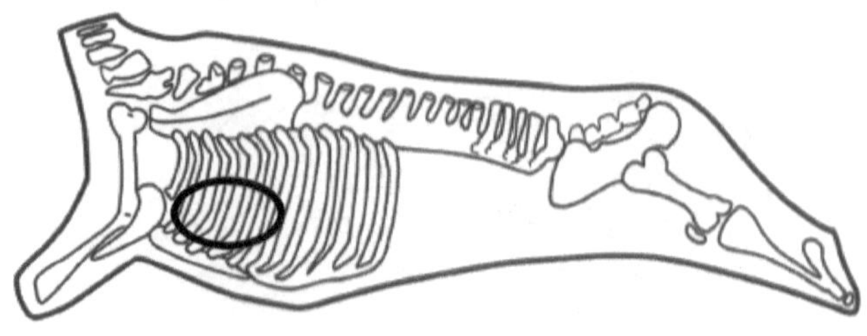

Tomahawk
LONGISSIMUS DORSI/SPINALIS DORSI

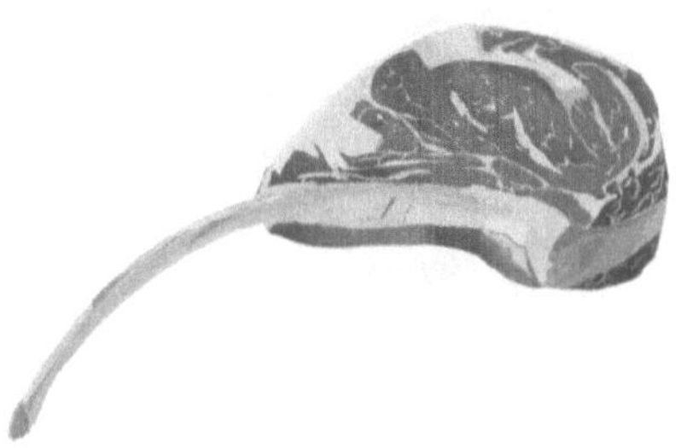

Tomahawk derived from the rib section of the bovine is essentially bone in rib-eye containing the cap and the loin, Longissimus and spinalis dorsi. This sub cut is rare and hard to obtain in a retail setting.

THE CUT

The tomahawk normally can be cut with a butcher knife carefully between each rib. Depending on the width of the cut can leave with a 3 - 4 Inch piece of meat weighing 3 - 4 pounds.

HOW TO SLICE

Remove loin following off the curved bone of Tomahawk. Slice the fat tail off to give a more conformed look of meat. Decipher the grain and slice against it.

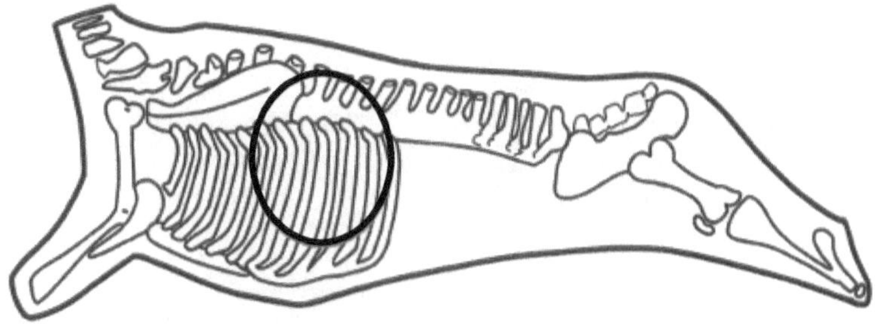

T-bone
LONGISSIMUS DORSI/PSOAS MAJOR

The T-bone is derived from the frontal area of the short loin of the bovine, front hip side being a sub-primal. T-bones majority of the meat comes from the longissimus dorsi (strip loin) with the opposing side containing a small amount of psoas major (tenderloin). T-bone is a staple steak for carnivores or OG grilles.

THE CUT

Bone saw individual steaks at least 1 ¼ inch followed by bone dusting off each sub cut. Removing intermuscular fat surrounding the short loin can be done before or after individual steaks are cut.

HOW TO SLICE

Remove a small portion of tenderloin and strip loin from the bone after preparation. Decipher the grain and slice against it.

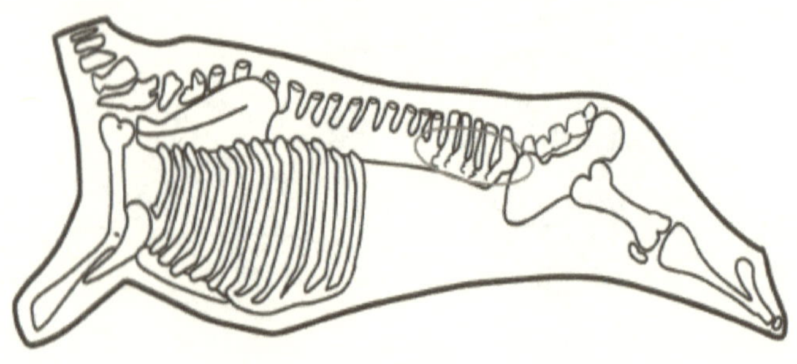

Tri-tip
TENSOR FASCIAE LATAE

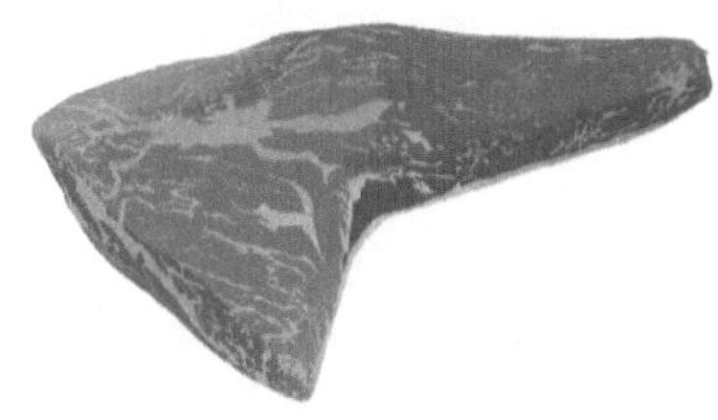

Tri-tip is a triangle shaped cut that is derived from the bottom sirloin subprimal. The cut has a rich buttery and beefy taste while containing intramuscular marbling to other meat cuts. Tri-tip is a cut more demanded on the west coast, you won't find this in New York. Tri-tip is a cut growing in popularity due to more exposure through cooking and barbecue competitions. Also can be named culotte (French) Newport steak, Santa Maria steak, and triangle steak.

THE CUT

During trimming the excess intramuscular fat is mostly removed from the meat opposite of the fat cap of the meat.

HOW TO SLICE

The grain changes about ¾ of the way through the sub cut. Visibly identify the grain direction and cut it again.

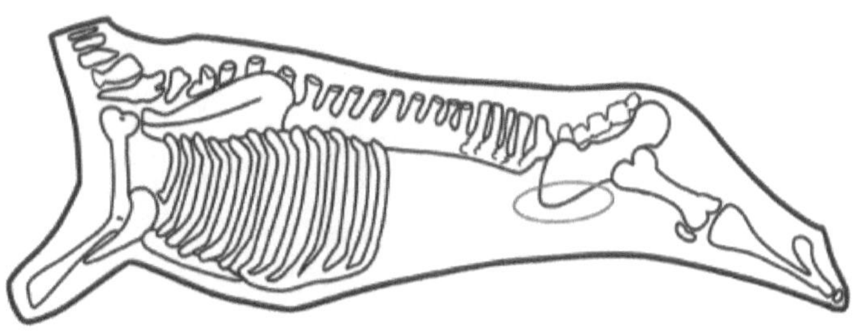

ABOUT THE AUTHORS

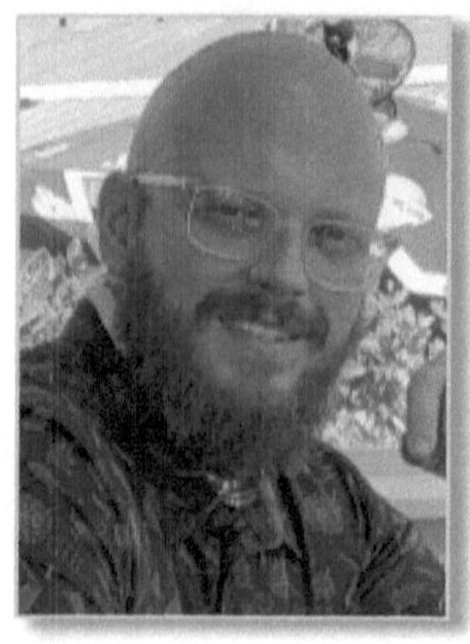

Adam G. Ellis is a Chef/Meat Cutter and Florida certified food manager. He has had wide experience in large corporate retail companies such as Best Buy, Penske, and Barnes and Noble. He also received his Certified Nursing Certificate at Cambridge College in 2012 and became licensed as a CNA in Florida the same year. He is *uniquely qualified* to have written this book, "A Surgical Approach to Meat Cutting," with his physician father, George F. Ellis, MD.

Adam was featured in 2021 as having created alternatives to the traditional Thanksgiving meal when there was a nationwide turkey shortage. He recently started a podcast with his colleagues, *Chewing the Fat*, which features stories about meat cutting and cooking. He enjoys relaxing with family and friends and developing new recipes that combine original ingredients into meats such as "Beer in Brats" and "Whiskey Brisket Burgers."

 **George F. Ellis**, MD is a Urological Surgeon and award-winning filmmaker. He is a published author, is a radio personality, and has been featured on several podcasts and other media venues. He has worked with hospitals, clinics, and large corporations in the private and public health sectors and now dedicates his medical expertise to the uninsured and homeless. Dr. Ellis' filmmaking has won wide recognition and several awards at film festivals worldwide, including the *"2023 Debut Filmmaker Award at the Dubai International Cine Carnival"*. An avid amateur chef, he has enjoyed watching his son, Adam, achieve advanced skills in the culinary arts and high levels of respect from his peers in the food industry. He enjoys spending time with family and friends at the beach and hiking in the Rocky Mountains. Find his work on IMDb, Facebook, Instagram, YouTube, and Filmfreeway.com/GeorgeEllis